KUNDALINĪ TANTRA
SONG OF LIBERATION

JAN ESMANN
FOREWORD BY DAVID SPERO

SIRIUS INK
www.siriusink.com

Kundalini Tantra

First edition printed by:

Sirius Productions, Wilsonville, Oregon, 97070, USA.

ISBN: 978-1-940964-02-7

Additional editing by Lila Sterling and Waldo Thompson.

Cover design by Jan Esmann and Lila Sterling.

Also by Jan Esmann:

Lovebliss – The Essence of Self-realization

This readable book clearly explains what Self-realization is and maps the road from ignorance to Self-realization and beyond. It includes new translations of three of the best Kashmir Shaivism classics dealing with the state of enlightenment and how to reach it.

Enlightenment 101 – From Ignorance to Grace

108 common fallacies about what enlightenment is are examined and a more correct view is proposed for each of them. In this context is explained the nature of the Self, how to reach it, and in particular the shaktipāt path.

The Artist's Craft

This is a 430 page handbook for the contemporary artist wishing to learn about the craft of painting. All aspects of technique are covered and there are numerous lessons for the chairoscuro painter and the colorist. Includes a complete list of pigments and commercial tube colors and their permanence.

Kundalini Tantra

Table of Contents

Kundalini Tantra

Foreword by David Spero

The human body-mind is a precious flower.

It arises out of Sat-Chit-Ananda (Absolute-Consciousness-Bliss), which designs its appearance and structure.

Both the human nervous system and universe in which it appears arise to express all the qualities of Sat-Chit-Ananda.

The human body-mind, forged out of the energetic frequencies of our planet and universe, arises as a Realizing Agent, in and as the field of Sat-Chit-Ananda.

Our universe creates Realizing Agents in order to comprehend its environment, as well as explore the native qualities of its own knowing and feeling processes.

Knowledge and feeling, in human subjectivity, create trajectories through which humans re-enter the Ground of Ecstatic Being.

The power of true and total Self-realization in human beings, in the Vedic sense of Upanishadic-style Unity Consciousness, appears as Consciousness is known within and without, free of relativity.

This range of recognition from the Self (within) to the Self (without) encompasses the legitimate and full epistemological territory of the human being's spiritual intelligence (in the field of sadhana or spiritual practice).

Experientially, earth-bound human body-minds arise in the wild and transformative atmosphere of the play of opposites, which encourage several potential, innate, human responses: the activity of Self-Inquiry into Being, Radiant Recognition of Being's Reflective Intensity and Energetic Participation in Vibratory Current.

In order to experience the Aboriginal Lila of Ecstatic Self-Recognition, a human being first learns to enjoy and relish the waves of spiritual surrender that happen within the ocean of opposites.

In due course, knowledge and experience of this relative ocean lead to full recognition and intuition of Sat-Chit-Ananda, which is experienced in its fullness as an Ocean of Liberated Bliss.

In human beings, Sat suggests a primary and immovable seat of

Silent Being, beyond all forms of cognition. Chit intimates Self-Reflecting Luminosity (of Being). Ananda arises as Limitless Happiness and Pure Energy, in which Self-Understanding (Chit) and Pure Being (Sat) mingle ferociously to produce sufficient Devotional Fire, which helps birth the Kundalini-Shakti Current.

Kundalini-Shakti, the Primal Life-Current, originates within the aboriginal womb of the universe. It arises as Adi-Parashakti, the Supreme Vibrational Energy, who is also Primal Devi, the Supreme Goddess. She extends Her Cosmic Limbs as Kundalini-Shakti throughout all aspects of the universe, relative and absolute.

Devi manifests this entire universe in Her Own Non-Dual Vibration. Later on, She organically stimulates and energizes, i.e. initiates, the spiritual processes in human beings through the Prana-Shakti Current.

Please note that the ways in which I've defined Sat-Chit-Ananda in this essay are non-exhaustive. Also, their meanings fluctuate within the context of each arising sentence, to some extent. Thus, at one time, Luminosity might be attributed to either Chit or Ananda. One could, therefore, with sufficiently deep realization and analysis, continue to explore further nuances of these terms, as well as the ways in which these ever-freshly discovered meanings interact.

Thus, still another way to formulate this universal concept of Sat-Chit-Ananda is one of Void-ness or Unmoved Silence, Mirror-Like Radiance and Ecstatic Bliss-Current.

Yet, thought and language fail to comprehend, on their own terms and levels, the wholeness of existence (the combined flavors of Emptiness, Radiance and Vitality); they nevertheless invite us into the most exquisite subjective banquet.

To eat of this banquet requires spiritual transmission from Realized Beings. Through compassion, such Beings dispense the various flavors of Sat-Chit-Ananda.

Being-Knowledge-Bliss thus are simultaneously the appearance of our universe, as well as its inner texture. It's also the actual, living texture of every body-mind, gross and subtle, organic and inorganic.

Monism insinuates the ultimate context of our universe. Without an accompanying monistic background, dualism remains the "big lie" of theology and metaphysics. There can be no conclusive and ultimate spiritual realization issuing from a dualistic system.

The only way to push into the most extreme forms of Heart-Awakening is by diving into the Unknowable Bliss of Pure Being with an open human heart.

Each human being's spiritual voyage is unique, manifesting from a life that is profoundly idiosyncratic. Human lives contain psychological/emotional ranges of light and darkness, pain and pleasure, the raw materials of spiritual evolution. Out of the friction born within the realm of opposites, the desire to know the Self is born, through Grace.

It's the degree of sincerity and passion of that exploratory process of realizing the Self, within the dualistic terrain of human experience, alongside a natural mode of Self-transcending activity (sadhana), which offers the possibility of true and lasting realization for human beings who otherwise remain held captive to the limitations of time and space.

To attempt to create a spiritual teaching out of such tragi-comic elements requires intuitionally easeful abandonment of the lies born of conventional knowledge and experience, which are invariably designed to dupe the natural spiritual intelligence of human beings.

Thus, required is a radical avoidance of the various traps

condoned by "traditional wisdom" and "conventional religion," as well as a fiery unwillingness to bend to the various authorities that embody a hyper-masculinized approach to life and spirituality. Such patriarchal lineages currently maintain a throbbing stranglehold on the consciousness of humanity.

Discarding the gigantic heap of repressive theological, spiritual and metaphysical lies, which attempt to trash bodily existence, one spontaneously begins to look into Reality directly, through the agency of the Shakti, where, suddenly, and for no reason at all, except perhaps the "reason" of love, there can be a gentle leap into the Heart of the Mother.

That leap occurs from inside a human body, which remains senior to all forms of subjective spiritual realizations. Organically divine from its outset, established beyond the pairs of opposites implicitly, by virtue of its very own Shakti, the body-mind flowers elegantly into Cosmic Realization.

According to this understanding, the human body-mind, house or container for all spiritual realizations, becomes endlessly saturated with Cosmic Bliss-Energy, until the very surface of the skin, along with the entire body-mind complex, dissolves in the elixir of Immortal, Nectarous Bliss that is Reality Itself and the

wholeness of the Enlightened Condition.
That Path is strewn with the leaves of Grace and Devotion.

Namaste,

David Spero

www.davidspero.org

Northern California, Oct. 23, 2013

Kundalini Tantra

INTRODUCTION

Kundalini Tantra

What is Tantra?

The origins of Tantra, or Tantrism, are obscure, but go at least 1500 years back if not much more. Today the word "Tantra" has become equated with pseudo-spiritual sexuality. That is a great shame, because Tantra is about so much more. Traditionally sexual practices were only a very small part of some off-shoot (left hand) branches of Tantra. The main thing about Tantra is that it focuses on Shakti, which is one aspect of the Self, the absolute. The other part is Shiva, or pure being. Shakti can be translated as the potential energy of the absolute, but one should understand that it is not separate from pure being and it is just as much being, consciousness and bliss as Shiva is. Shakti is identified as the Divine Mother. Shiva, the Divine Father. Tantrics are devoted to the Divine Mother. The Divine Mother resides in you as kundalinī and tantrics worship kundalinī and do their best to awaken kundalinī and merge it with Shiva in the brain. Tantra is concerned with practice (yoga) and the practicalities of getting enlightened. The finest tantric initiation is known as shaktipāt since it directly awakens the dormant kundalinī so it begins to work on your enlightenment from within and automatically. There are numerous tantric techniques that aim at awakening kundalinī, in fact all tantric techniques can be said to have that aim, but shaktipāt is the descent of divine grace that will awaken kundalinī so it will smoothly and rapidly take the yogi to enlightenment. Shaktipāt is a very rare initiation as very few have the power and ability to give it and the state of enlightenment necessary to give

17

it. I had the good fortune to become Self-realized and for some reason I can give shaktipāt and those two combined by definition makes me a tantric teacher. This book is a modern day tantric book. It seeks to expound what Self-realization is about, but also what the Divine Mother is about. The Divine Mother is to be understood as a loving term to denote the Shakti aspect of the Self and its presence in one once kundalinī shakti has been awakened through shaktipāt. With shaktipāt all other yogas become realized in the seeker, this includes bhakti yoga, the yoga of devotion. The kundalinī shaktipāt yogi tends to be devoted to the Divine Mother, since the divine feminine seems an appropriate form with which to grasp the wonderful grace that grabs one after shaktipāt gets one's kundalinī going for good and uncompromisingly works for one's liberation. In this book you will find the kundalinī awakened by shaktipāt described as Mother's Grace. In fact, the working title of this book was "Mother's Grace". However, since very few would be able to relate to that title, we decided to change it.

Love,

Jan Esmann, October 2013

TEACHINGS

Kundalini Tantra

How to Meditate

The most important practices are the following:
1. Kundalinī kriyā meditation.
2. Kundalinī prānāyāma.
3. Chakra kriyā meditation.

After these have been described, a few other practices will also be described, but do kundalinī kriyā meditation daily. Meditate 45 minutes twice daily and you will soon get results.

Common to all Practices

Warm-up, 5 min.

Sit comfortably in an upright posture. Go through your body beginning with the feet and ending with the head. Feel your feet, but in such a manner that you do not do it from your head down, but rather are present in the feet and let the feet feel themselves. Let your whole attention be filled with the sensation of the feet. Then proceed to the ankles, the calves, and so forth. Spend as much time each place as is needed to feel the presence there. When you reach the head then feel the entire body in toto. Notice the body is breathing by itself. Do not interfere with the rhythm, simply observe it. Then proceed to the meditation.

Ending meditation

When it's time to end meditation, don't just stop and get up. First of all let go and see if you don't go deeper by letting go. Spend some time like this. Then when you really want to stop, sit with closed eyes a while and then slowly open them while staying in meditation. Or if you don't want to open them slowly, open and close your eyes a few times while trying to hold the meditative state. Then meditate a few minutes with open eyes. Note how your state is different now than from it was just before you began meditating. Remember: We do not go out of meditation, because meditation is merging with the Self and we don't want to go out of the Self. Rather we take meditation into the waking state.

Kundalinī Kriyā Meditation

The practice consists of three methods you switch between. When you reach a plateau, you switch to one of the other methods and when that reaches a plateau you switch again, and so forth. All the time with one objective: To intensify Shakti more and more and merge with it.

1. Body breathing

As you observe the breathing, feel the entire body. Feel your energetic presence in and around the body. Now feel on the in-breath that you expand, that the energy field grows more intense and becomes larger. On the out-breath simply let go. Another way of saying it is that on the in-breath you feel the Shakti growing in intensity and size. On the out-breath you let go of any control and duality and merge with Shakti in and around the body. As this continues you will feel the body's limits dissolve and that the feeling of Shakti becomes more tangible than the feeling of the physical body. Do this as long as Shakti gets stronger and you merge more and more; when it reaches a plateau switch to spine breathing.

2. Spine breathing

On the in-breath feel you are moving energy up the entire spine at once, from the perineum to the brain. On the out-breath feel you are radiating energy or lovebliss, in all directions from the brain. With a little practice you will feel the energy moving up the spine and radiating from the brain on both the in- and out-breath. You can visualize a flower stem up the spine, and the crown of the flower in the brain if it helps. Do this as long as Shakti gets stronger and you merge more and more. When it reaches a plateau, go to the next practice.

3. Inflow-outflow

For this you do not need to follow your breath. The instruction is simple: Sense shakti, grace, love, or however you want to relate to it, flow into the body and radiate from the body simultaneously. If you can get it to flow into the entire spine and radiate from the entire spine simultaneously, so much the better.

4. Merging in lovebliss

When you experience being filled with Shakti or lovebliss, then let go of your methods and merge with it. This is the goal of all practices and methods, so no matter what practice you are doing, if you are on the verge of transcending I-ness and merging, then let go of the method/practice and merge in lovebliss.

Kundalinī Prāṇāyāma

This is in the class of prāṇāyāmas, meaning breathing exercises. But the focus of the practice is not control of prāṇa (vital-force), but awakening and arousal of kundalinī. The purpose of this is to generate Shakti-bliss on which one can surf into the Self and merge awareness and Shakti into pure being.

Sit in a comfortable position and do the preparations for meditation as described above.

There is a special breathing cycle to this that it is important to keep. It has three steps: Breathing in, holding the breath and breathing out. It is important that all of the three phases are of equal duration. It is also important to keep the rhythm going steadily at the same pace, so one should find a duration that suits one well. One could count to three repeatedly in the same rhythm (or whatever number is appropriate). It is important not to get tense, so one should find a comfortable number and rhythm one can keep steadily for 45 minutes without getting out of breath or feeling one is enforcing control over the breath. Enforcing control will not do any good at all, in fact it will block the intended result. It should be a nice, calm, peaceful cycle.

1. On the in-breath, imagine and feel shakti moving from the perineum and up the entire spine to the top of the head. Imagine it as a point going up, or as a flow in the entire channel. One can visualize a flower stem up the spine with the crown in the brain; or a garden hose or a neon tube or whatever if one feels it helps.

2. Hold your breath in a comfortable and relaxed manner. Meanwhile, imagine/feel the energy in the brain radiate in all directions.

3. On the out-breath, continue radiating shakti in all directions from the brain.

Soon you will find that shakti moves up the spine and radiates from the brain at the same time, and does so on the in-breath while holding the breath and on the out-breath. That is a good sign and you should keep with that.

Do this for as long as you like. 30-45 minutes is a nice period. Do repeated periods if you have time and the urge.

Soon you will experience great bliss.

Be aware that this practice is for awakening and arousing kundalinī. You may experience this as something moving in your spine, but do not be alarmed. If you find it releases more energy than you are comfortable with then also do not be alarmed, for it will soon calm down and integrate with the system. If it becomes too much, stop and do meditation 1 of kundalinī kriyā.

Chakra Kriyā Meditation

This is a dynamic way of opening all the chakras. Below I will describe how it is done with one chakra, but the full meditation takes all the chakras one at a time from the bottom to the top and then back down.

A. Pulsating. On the in-breath sense energy going forward from the spine and to the front of the body and on the out-breath moving back into the spine. Do this for about ten breaths. (If working with the root chakra or crown chakra, sense the energy moving up on the in-breath and down on the out-breath)

B. Expanding. Sense the ball of light in chakra. On the in-breath sense it expanding and on the out-breath simply let go. Do this for about ten breaths.

C. Sense it radiating from the chakra in all directions on both the in-breath and out-breath.

D. Sense energy radiating into the chakra from all directions on both the in- and out-breath. Or sense it radiating from and radiating into the chakra at the same time.

E. Sense energy moving up from the chakra to the next chakra on the in-breath and down again on the out-breath.

A-E is one cycle for the chakra, repeat for each chakra in turn. First move from the bottom to the top, then down again one chakra at a time.

As you do this practice, you may feel pressure in the body in the chakra areas. Also hidden emotions may arise. Please allow whatever comes up to arise, be what it is and leave. Remember the goal is not catharsis, but to generate a pulse of shakti (spiritual energy), on which you can surf into bliss and Self.

27

Other Methods

Sit in a comfortable position and do the preparations for meditation as described above.

Root and Crown Union

This meditation has several stages to be performed in the following order:

A. Feel the perineum (area between genitals and anus) and sense that on the in-breath energy moves up a few inches and on the out-breath moves down again. Do this for about ten breaths.

B. Sense a ball of energy an inch or so above the perineum. On the in-breath expand it and on the out-breath simply let go. Do this for about ten breaths.

C. Sense energy radiating in all directions from this root center just above the perineum. Try to get a sense of continuous flow. Do this for as long as you go deeper and deeper - or if possible merge in bliss. When you reach a plateau, go to D.

D. Now center your attention on the top of the scull. On the in-breath and also on the out-breath sense you are allowing the energy to rush up your spine to the crown. Do this for about ten breaths.

E. On the in-breath sense energy rising about an inch out through the top of your scull. On the out-breath, sense it going down again about two inches into the head. Do this for about ten breaths.

F. Sense a ball of energy at the scull, about two inches in diameter. On the in-breath expand it and on the out-breath simply let go. Do this for about ten breaths.

G. Sense energy radiating in all directions from the crown. Try to get a sense of continuous flow. Do this for as long as you go deeper and deeper, or if possible merge in bliss. When you reach a plateau, go to A and repeat the steps.

At a point you will sense both the root chakra and the crown chakra radiating at once. Then go into that and ignore the above steps. As you go deeper, you will sense the two chakras are not separate and you might get a peculiar sense that they are not separate in space. Go into that. When out of it, again return to the above steps.

Four Kinds of Witnessing During Meditation

"Witnessing" designates a special state of consciousness or pure awareness where you are detached from something and observe it from a place that is untouched by it. Usually this something is a state of consciousness with which you were hitherto identified. The value of witnessing is threefold: First witnessing is the natural stance of the enlightened one, so temporary witnessing is a short experience of what it is like to be Self-realized. Second, it is liberating from the drama of life to stand outside of it and witness it. Third there is catharsis in witnessing some drama one was hitherto identified with and thus, with the witnessing, has become free of with a release of emotional charge.

First type of witnessing concerns the mind. It is not necessarily first in a hierarchical epistemological order, but because it is often the first kind of witnessing people become conscious of experiencing; so it is merely the first worth mentioning in the order of how witnessing presents itself to a typical meditator. Once this kind of witnessing sets in, you will observe thoughts and impulses in the mind, that you would normally have taken to be you, as distinctly not you. The mind may become quiet, or it may become agitated, but that matters not since you are a detached observer to its contents and stirrings. The content of the mind may be banal or profound, it matters not in the least, for it is definitely not you and the important part of the experience is not the content of the mind, but the fact that you so distinctly experience it is not you. It is similar to looking in a mirror: You recognize yourself, but know it is not you. In witnessing, even the notion that it resembles yourself is lost. You recognize that you once assumed it was you, but also that you no longer assume that at all. You are a witness, neither more nor less. One other significant aspect of this type of witnessing is that you become a witness to the observer of consciousness. Yes, the observer is not the witness! The observer is a natural stance the mind can adopt, but it is still within the mind, or rather, based on identification. The point from which you witness is devoid of any kind of identification whatsoever. So first you step into the observer, then you witness the identification inherent in the observer and step into pure being, which is the only true witnessing stance.

Second type of witnessing concerns the emotions; the heart. This for some reason often comes after a period of witnessing the mind. Suddenly you become detached from some emotion and simply observe it (witness it). Such an emotion may be the ecstasy of immature samādhi, or it may be any banal emotion such as fear or joy. Usually detachment from the mind precedes this type of witnessing, but I am not sure it should always be so. You may witness the mind, or at least part of it, and there may be some joy in this witnessing, some pride perhaps. It takes a little experience of mind-witnessing to suddenly step out of this subtle pleasure and witness this pleasure also. It is for some reason more acceptable for people to admit they are not the thoughts in the mind. After all, anyone can think contradictory thoughts and thoughts they do not agree with; thus they can easily realize they are not their thoughts, but rather are the master or observer of the thoughts. But when it comes to emotions, people are more reluctant to disidentify from them. People are less in control of their emotions and they are generally driven by unconscious impulses. Thus there is something terrifying to many in witnessing emotions. Not only do you distance yourself from the manifest emotion, but you implicitly distance yourself from the unconscious sense of self from which the emotions spring. Distancing oneself from the mind is fairly easy, but distancing oneself from emotions is a little more difficult.

Third type of witnessing concerns the body. Not only the flesh, but in particular the field permeating and surrounding the body, which any experienced meditator will recognize immediately as a truer sense of presence in time and space than the physical body alone. The sense of being the body is more deeply-rooted than the sense of being the emotions. After all, the emotions can change and be manipulated: you can change boredom to happiness and anger to love, but the body just stays the same (more or less). So it is easier to witness emotions than to witness body-identification. Just as it is easier to witness thoughts than to witness identification with emotions. Yet it is clearly possible to be a witness to not only the physical body, but to the field that permeates the body and reaches beyond it. Identification with the body first is identification with this field, then secondarily identification with the flesh. However, people generally have it the other way around since they don't sense this field and only know the flesh. Most people's field is hardly larger than the body, but any experienced kundalinī-kriyā meditator will instantly recognize what I am talking about, when I say your bodily presence is a field that permeates the body and extends some distance around it. This field can become very large, as in the case of a kundalinī shaktipāt master, where it can easily fill an entire room, or it can just be an inch larger than the body as in the case of a neophyte meditator without an awakened kundalinī. Once your kundalinī is awakened, if you meditate daily on shakti, your sense of this field will soon expand to about two or three feet around the body. Witness this. It is one thing to witness the physical body - in fact that is quite easy: anyone can imagine having lost a hand or a leg and still observe their presence in time and space. But to witness this metaphysical presence in and around the physical body is something quite different altogether. We are talking about being detached from your physical body and being detached from your metaphysical presence in time and space. This usually comes after detachment from the emotions and detachment from the mind. When this detachment and witnessing comes, you are literally located nowhere. There is no point anywhere at all which you can refer to as you. You are a witness to everything. This state is by nature very serene; though it may also be either just empty void or bliss; that depends on how far one's meditation has progressed. With more experience it becomes more blissful. Only to the neophyte is it a scary void.

A fourth level of witnessing comes when you begin to see the Self in everything as Shakti and lovebliss. You then witness the physical universe as an "overlay" on the Divine. You sense the impersonal Divine creative impulse or intelligence or love behind everything; this is of course Shakti and you sense a oneness with this. That makes you a witness to creation, to everything manifest, in fact to everything around you. This is the beginning of non-duality, of Advaita. The plurality of creation begins to go away and you sense a oneness of Shakti in and as everything. There is still a duality of Self and other, but other is seen as one. In Self-realization, or what the neo-Advaitins call "non-duality", there is a duality between inner and outer, and outer is seen as a plurality; so is the mind. In bliss consciousness, where this fourth kind of witnessing belongs, there are only two, two and nothing but two, no plurality: There is the unmanifest, which you are, and then there is the Shakti which appears as many outside you. Hence you witness everything. You are a witness to creation. Creation sustained by one Divine principle, which is love, bliss and Shakti in one.

Kundalinī and Shaktipāt

When ordinarily searching for the Self, there is very little help. However, help is there, waiting to be discovered. One can become overwhelmed by the amount of practices and paths that claim to lead one to the Self. This may lead one to think there is an abundance of help in reaching the Self. However, there is virtually no help and one has to make it on one's own. The reason is: all practices have to be given up. No practice will lead you to the Self. You have to give up practices and stand on your own, then give that up also. It is a frustrating fact of spiritual life that one is trying to get to something that one has no idea what is, nor how to find; so one clings to practices and methods.

Faith in teachings is another trap. If you have too much faith in teachings, you become attached to them and cannot let go. The Self is indescribable, so no teaching will ever be able to catch or describe it, no matter how erudite or simple the teaching may be. So, apparently there is nothing left but to give up? If one can truly and utterly give up, that might be a way, but for most people giving up is not an option. One may give up for a while, but problems and questions have a way of sneaking in on one again and then effort is back.

The ultimate question is: Who am I? Everyone asks that question in one form or another at various times in life. Some are obsessed with the question and they are the real seekers. Many are satisfied with the answers the mind can provide and they go to workshops, seminars and therapists for answers. Others are never satisfied and they are the real seekers. Many find building up a personality is the answer. Others know that no matter what personality, it will always be a lie about who you really are; they are the real seekers.

Though there is virtually no help for the final jump into the Self, there is plenty of help on the way. In fact, too much since one may become so fundamentally confused, one may despair. So many methods! What to choose? However, one special kind of help stands out from the mass. That is shaktipāt. Shaktipāt is not a means, a system or a practice; therefore it does not fall in the category of conflicting advice and dogma. Shaktipāt is Divine grace passing through a qualified master to a qualified student for the sake of granting the student Self-realization and god-consciousness. Kundalinī awakened though shaktipāt will not only lead you on the path, but it will take you past the final jump into Self-realization. Shaktipāt is grace and the actions of an awakened kundalinī are grace.

The master may do his best for any random student to receive shaktipāt, but the truth of the matter is that though the master may be a fine channel for Divine grace, it is not certain that Divine grace will flow to the student. In other words: though the master may be able and willing to give it, it is not sure the student is ready or capable of receiving it or holding on to it. Some get it who have not even asked for it, others ask and ask and will only get it after years of patient waiting. It is mysterious. The real master will know if someone is ready or not, but will seldom say anything about it in order to not disillusion the student or make him or her give up hope. A certain readiness is required. A certain purity of heart and mind must be there for the Shakti to enter and grab hold of the student; also a lack of rigidity.

It is a bit like unscrewing a screw; if the screw has rusted into the wood, you can't get it out. Or maybe the person wants the screw out and the screw is loose enough, but the person does not want to lose whatever the screw is holding in place, so he or she unconsciously fights the unscrewing. Or maybe the ignorance held in place by the screw is so smart it screws the screw back in whenever you turn it out. Or maybe the screw is ready to be removed and the ignorance held in place ready to fall off. Such is the happy meeting between a shaktipāt master and disciple. Practices may help prepare the disciple for the "unscrewing"; on the other hand, they may become an attachment and thus hinder the "unscrewing". So how do you prepare for shaktipāt? You don't! You just pray and hope you are ready for it. But in general you have to be pure and gentle of nature. Long for God or Self and be unselfish. Be kind to others. Don't be arrogant. And don't be attached to any sādhana or spiritual belief system you may have been involved in; be ready to give it up. Be humble in all respects. What matters is quality of heart and purity of soul. And what really matters is surrender. Surrender! This is such a mysterious quality you will have to learn about it from inner experience.

When someone receives shaktipāt, it is more a question of the master experiencing the Shakti in him grab the student. The master does not do much. Shakti is all-knowing and knows when the student is ready; the master is one who has surrendered completely to Shakti, so he just lets it happen. However, it is not that the master is a mere channel; he has to have an awakened kundalinī and have surrendered to Shakti to such a degree, that he has become Self-realized. So Self-realization is a matter of surrender? Yes, indeed. You surrender to the Self! The wonderful realization on the shaktipāt path is that one realizes that Shakti and the Self are one. In the beginning one feels like Shakti is working on one, not realizing that the Shakti is the Self, but later, when one merges with Shakti more and more often, one realizes Shakti and the Self are one and the same.

The body is a repository of sacred energy, known as kundalinī. Kundalinī is Shakti that has individualized into you as an ignorant person. This means that undoing you as an ignorant person is a matter of undoing kundalinī. Kundalinī has manifested you; kundalinī contains the blueprint of your ignorant structure and thus within it contains the knowledge of how to undo your ignorance and make you enlightened. This undoing is known as merging kundalinī with Shiva. This merging happens in the brain. Before it happens though, kundalinī has to awaken and journey from its hiding place in the root chakra up through the spine and into the brain. Kundalinī can awaken in three ways: spontaneously, through practices or through grace. Shaktipāt awakens kundalinī and belongs to the category of grace. Once awakened by grace, it is wise to support kundalinī's unfoldment with practices. Similarly, if kundalinī awakens spontaneously or through practice, it is wise to support it with shaktipāt.

After shaktipāt, during practice, one will experience kriyās. Kriyās are spontaneous manifestations of kundalinī shakti and can be body movements, inner visions, sounds uttered, etc. Do not be alarmed by kriyās; they are in all cases a manifestation of kundalinī shakti cleaning and improving the system. After shaktipāt one's sādhana becomes automatic. One practices to allow Shakti to work in and on one, and also to support kundalinī shakti's journey rising up the spine.

Kundalinī is not simply energy, it is really your pure being. As such, enlightenment is inherent in kundalinī. Kundalinī is the immense power of consciousness and it may scrutinize dark places in your system. This may be painful for a time, but bliss lies behind it all the while and will eventually break through. You cannot get fully enlightened without kundalinī shakti. Many maintain this is not the case, but I say from experience it is. You can reach basic Self-realization without kundalinī, but to move on you have to have an awakened kundalinī and merge Shiva and Shakti. Self-realization without Shakti is dull and lifeless; with Shakti you are full of supreme devotion and love. Kundalinī will take you all the way to the Self, to God. It is not some occult energy, as some claim, it is love Divine.

If you want to enjoy the emotion and fullness of life, you will have to travel the path of kundalinī shakti. Others emphasize the stillness and emptiness of Brahman, the void, but they only have half the truth. Shakti is not some human event, it is the Divine laughter in creation, it is supreme devotion and it contains the stillness and emptiness of Brahman, but also the flow of life in supreme devotion and supreme bliss. Those who have only merged in the stillness of Brahman, the void, do not understand kundalinī shakti, they only recognize the void within themselves. Those who have Shakti in their sādhana and have realized Shakti, recognize the Divine in not only the Self, but in everything around them also.

Technically, when the master gives shaktipāt, he goes into oneness with the recipient. He not only is in internal oneness within himself, but he has to be able to go into oneness with someone else and so to speak pull the other into bliss and pure being.

It is a general impression that kundalinī can be awakened with various hatha yoga practices like concentration, prānāyāmas or bandhas. However, this is generally not so, as can be concluded by the innumerable amount of people doing these practices and the small amount of them who actually succeed in awakening kundalinī. It is also a general impression, that a competent master can awaken kundalinī in anybody by a mere touch, or glance. This is also not so; the recipient has to be ripe for a kundalinī awakening to occur even through shaktipāt. But yogic meditation practices will help prepare the way for a kundalinī awakening to happen. Shaktipāt will do so by directly awakening the sleeping kundalinī; prānāyāmas and bandhas do so by cleansing the spinal channel and also arousing kundalinī; asanas (postures) have hardly any effect on awakening kundalinī but keep the body fit. Spiritually I consider asanas a waste of time; it is nice gymnastics but nothing more. The same with tai chi and qi-gong which can never take you to Self-realization since they only work with the etheric body. It is better to use the time meditating if you want to get Self-realized.

It is not known why some are disposed for kundalinī awakening and some are not. Sure, practices will help and strong visualization of an awakened kundalinī combined with a genuine longing for kundalinī to awaken is the most potent aid for an awakening; but again: how many have such a strong longing? Also this can be developed; with strong visualization repeated day after day with love.

An aroused kundalinī is not an awakened kundalinī. An aroused kundalinī will give some sensations of pressure at the root chakra and also lights in the head and bliss, etc. but this cannot be compared to the radical shift in kundalinī's activity when kundalinī is fully awakened. With the awakening of kundalinī begins a whole new kind of process in the body that aims at transforming consciousness from ignorance to Self-realization and god-consciousness.

One must not think of kundalinī as a weird occult force. It is the force that keeps the body and mind going every second of the day, only in a limited form. The awakening of kundalinī is merely the removal of the restrictions. The energy released continuously from a sleeping kundalinī is what upholds the functions of the mind and body and allows regular learning, but once awakened, the energy released will act as an evolutionary force transforming the regular consciousness to an enlightened one.

The transformation is not finished until kundalinī has dissolved itself in the awakened brain. The brain is the seat of the crown chakra (sahasrāra) and kundalinī not only opens this chakra, but also dissolves into the pure being accessible there. This is traditionally known as the merging of Shakti with Shiva. This is a revolution in human consciousness and awareness beyond mere Self-realization.

The awakened kundalinī will purify the energy channels of the body, the nādis, and this may lead to spontaneous movements of the body, called "kriyās". Kriyās can also be mental or emotional. At first it may seem odd that a sādhana and mystical process designed to give liberation results in weird movements of the arms, body and spine, but on second thought it just proves how profound the process is. Other systems try to purify the nādis through postures, prānāyāmas and bandhas, thus forcing the prāna shakti into the nādis in order to cleanse them. The shaktipāt kriyās are a result of the shakti automatically entering the nādis and purifying them. Thus shaktipāt sādhana is the most supreme sādhana since it fulfills the goal of all other sādhanas automatically and effortlessly.

It is noteworthy that the source of human evolution lies more or less dormant in every human being, and is fully awakened in a few lucky souls. For the person living with an awakened kundalini it is only all too obvious that he or she is in the midst of a process of accelerated evolution. Kundalini is a super intelligent force driving the evolution of consciousness. Spiritual evolution is clearly a result of an active or awakened kundalini.

Undoubtedly the state of samādhi is either a result of changed brain activity or samādhi forces the brain to behave differently; but either way there must be neurological correlates of the spiritual changes happening along with the process of kundalini arousal. Probably the nervous system of man is evolving in such a way as to allow samādhi to occur more and more frequently; certainly this was the conviction of Bucke as expressed in his old book Cosmic Consciousness and by Gopi Krishna in his many books. I tend to agree.

The first result of a kundalini awakened through shaktipāt is kriyās. The second, but most important, aspect is samādhi. Samādhi is a state where awareness has freed itself from identification with the small self and merged into the pure being of the Self. This merging is extremely blissful. Usually a bright light fills the brain and a kind of prolonged super-orgasm takes place in the body. The super-orgasmic state is a sign of immature samādhi, after a while it changes to a deep, silent bliss.

The inner light is a common feature of all mystical experiences in all cultures and ages. The Christian mystics speak of the illuminating glory of God and saint Symeon identified the blazing inner light with Christ and the Self. The Taoists speak of circulating light. Hindus speak of the blazing radiance of a multitude of suns that characterizes Brahman (the Self) or the self-luminous Ātman (Self). Sufis speak of "Noor": The splendor emanating from Divinity. We speak of enlightenment.

The ecstasy, or cosmic orgasm, that takes place the first times kundalinī reaches the brain, changes with practice to a soft, calm and quiet bliss. Ecstasy has to be transcended and the cosmic orgasms are in no way a goal in themselves. This is where so many western so called "tantrics" go astray. The goal is not ecstasy or sexual bliss, but samādhi. Sex will never lead to samādhi. Samādhi is a state where the awareness has been pulled out of the senses and merged with the Self.

Visions of various kinds may arise before the inner eye, but the most common are various dots of light. Of these the blue pearl is the most precious; it is the gateway to the Divine, to the pure Self. Some see a cobra dancing before their inner eye, which is a sign kundalinī has awakened. Every person will have his own inner experiences and kriyās.

The Crown Chakra

It is a new age myth that the crown chakra has to do with mental operations. You don't become more intellectual once the crown chakra opens. The crown chakra has to do with transpersonal states of consciousness. It is normally closed. It opens in three steps. At least this is how it happened for me. For others it may be different, but it seems to follow this pattern.

The first step is an opening the size of a very large coin or a tennis ball on the top of the head. With this opening you may begin to get somewhat access to temporary ecstatic and trans-ecstatic samādhi of union with the Self in meditation, but for many nothing special follows.

The second step is when the upper half of the brain opens up, so to speak. That is all the way down to the top of the ears and it feels like a small helmet or cap of glowing light has been put onto your head. When this happens you experience lovebliss and you may glide in and out of samādhi on a daily basis. It is tempting to think this is a fully opened crown chakra, but it is only halfway there.

Third step is when the entire underside of the brain opens up. A fully opened crown chakra is a complete ball of radiating white light. At one and the same time you sense energy radiating up into the brain from the spine, and simultaneously you sense energy radiating down from the brain. It radiates from the brain in all directions at once. Up, to the sides and down, like a small sun. Once this happens you are in a permanent samādhi of constant oneness with the Self and utter detachment from all identifications. You will begin to see a faint golden light in everything around you. This light is recognition of the Self in everything, but there could be other aspects to it as well. Funnily enough, the lovebliss will abate somewhat and turn into a silent, unmoving joy and love. Rather than you being in lovebliss, you will begin to see that everything is in lovebliss. All traces of ecstasy have gone.

Each step will open up in a matter of seconds or minutes. It is not that you move from step one to step two by having the coin-sized opening gradually expand; no, it comes in a rush when you are ready. In a matter of a minute or so, the coin-sized opening will expand down to the ears and you will experience hundreds of tiny "explosions" inside the brain signifying the "petals" of the chakra unfolding. Also the brain will become warm and you are most likely to see inner light. The most important and significant part is the hundreds of small "explosions" inside the brain because that is the chakra opening. Final opening will also happen in a matter of seconds as the underside of the half-open chakra folds downwards and meets at the stem of the spine. In my case it took about 25 years between step one and step two; and seven years between step two and step three. But that is just an example.

Meditation on the crown chakra is very important and the basic practice of bringing energy up the spine and into the brain, and radiating it from the brain in all directions, will help in this.

Types of Samādhi

The classical samādhi distinction is between savikalpa samādhi and nirvikalpa samādhi. Savikalpa means with fluctuations and nirvikalpa without fluctuations. In other words: Is something going on in the mind or not? However, this distinction is far from adequate. It is okay within a rigid system that teaches mind control, such as Patanjali's classic kriyā yoga, as a means to Self-realization, but once kundalinī is awakened and active, things become more complex. Then you have ecstasies and inner lights going on and off. The following samādhis, mentioned by Patanjali, overlap.

Patanjali's Samādhis:

Samprajnāta samādhi

This samādhi is of the mind and of I AM-ness. It is not very deep, though many never go beyond this. "Samprajnata" means "with cogitation". One does not really know the Self in this samādhi, since one is still in the mind and at best resting in I AM.

Asamprajnāta samādhi

"A" negates "with cogitation", so this samādhi is free of mind-stuff, meaning the mind is quiet, but one still rests only in I AM (at best).

Savitarka samādhi

"Savitarka" means with thought constructs. In this samādhi cogitation fuses and the object of meditation and its meaning fuse into a homogeneous unity. This is pure concept.

Nirvitarka samādhi

Here everything is gone but the object of meditation. One still does not abide in the Self. There is no active memory or thought processes. Only the mantra or flame, or whatever object one has for meditation, exists in awareness.

Savicāra and nirvicāra samādhi

These samādhis are similar to savitarka and nirvitarka samādhi. Patanjali says the difference is that these are with a subtle condition, meaning one abides in I AM with or without mind stuff.

Nirbīja samādhi

"Nirbīja" means "without seed". It refers to when the seed of I-ness is transcended and one abides in the Self.

Kaivalya

"Kaivalya" means "isolation". It occurs when you lose the object of meditation and abide in the Self alone. In the beginning one loses consciousness when entering kaivalya, but later one can remain conscious. Kaivalya is a type of nirivikalpa samādhi (see below).

Dharmamegha samādhi

When kaivalya is a permanent, natural state, it is known as dharmamegha samādhi. "Megha" means cloud and the cloud concerns "dharma". "Dharma" here does not refer to righteous action, virtue or religious duty. It refers to the mass of tendencies, impressions and karma accumulated by the yogi and which propels the yogi's life in a certain direction. In dharmamegha samādhi one has reached freedom from that accumulated mass and one abides permanently in the Self.

Patanjali's many samādhis are overlapping and a bit tedious. I prefer a modified version of the basic distinction between savikalpa and nirvikalpa samādhi:

Savikalpa samādhi

Non-luminous without ecstasy

It is a samādhi where the mind is full of thoughts and there are numerous feelings going on. But you are not identified with the thoughts and emotions and are thus somewhat a witness to them. You do not need an awakened kundalinī shakti to experience this.

Non-luminous with ecstasy

In the best savikalpa samādhis, those with shakti, you experience ecstasy; the eyelids flicker, the heart beats extra fast and violently, thoughts rush through the mind and breathing becomes deep and rapid. Ecstasy is a sign of an aroused kundalinī. However, kundalinī has not reached the brain since it is non-luminous.

Luminous without ecstasy

In this samādhi your brain becomes filled with white light and you are in calm semi-bliss. Inner light is a sign of an aroused kundalinī shakti and also a sign that some amount of shakti has reached the brain. It is not so often you have this; you usually have light and ecstasy together.

Luminous with ecstasy

In this samādhi, there is inner light, but also ecstasy: the eyelids flicker, the heart beats extremely fast, one perspires, thoughts run wild and one's breathing becomes deep and rapid; yet you are a calm witness to all this.

Turyā

In this samādhi you rest in the Self temporarily and from there witness the mind and emotions unfold. It may be with mental and emotional agitation or without; usually it is without. Most contemporary neo-Advaita teachers are stuck here and teach it is the highest.

Nirvikalpa samādhi

Nirvikalpa samādhi really means that you are in a state without fluctuations, however, there can still be (a few) fluctuations in the mind, they are just not you and you are a witness to them. You are temporarily established in pure being, in turyātīta, which lies beyond turyā.

1. Nirvikalpa (immature)

In this samādhi you become unconscious and do not have any sense of time. You meditate a short while, then suddenly meditate again and feel only a few minutes have passed, yet when you look at the watch a long time has passed without any sense of it. You will be in a state of bliss after this. However, unconsciousness is not the highest state.

2. Nirvikalpa (mature)

In this samādhi you rest in a state of unmanifest, pure being, which is the same state as that of the immature, unconscious nirvikalpa samādhi, yet now from there you consciously observe the sporadic thoughts and emotions. You are a witness to these since you are the void and are entirely without fluctuations. It is blissful. The pure being that you are one with is realized as "self-referential" and self-contained. It lacks nothing and wants nothing. The description of this samādhi sounds like turyā, I know, but it is different. Because of the similarity in description, many who experience turyā think it is nirvikalpa. Turyā is not "self-referential" so to speak, it is just a witness. The nir-vikalpa (non-fluctuation) quality of this samādhi refers to the absolute pure being of the Self, which is unmanifest and hence without fluctuations.

Sahaja samādhi

"Sahaja" means "spontaneous" or "natural". When established in the Self one is constantly in samādhi, this is called sahaja samādhi; thus there is a sahaja samādhi of Self-realization, one of god-consciousness and one of unity consciousness. However, some claim sahaja samādhi refers to a state of enlightenment that comes after unity consciousness. This is how David Spero uses it. Both definitions are valid, so just be sure what people mean.

Kundalini Tantra

TEXTS

Advaita Vedānta – A Short and Critical Presentation

Advaita Vedānta is an old Indian system of thought that has gained much popularity in the West. Literally "Vedānta" means "end of wisdom" and this immodest name implies that Vedānta contains the highest spiritual teachings. In one sense it does, in one sense it does not, as we will see. "Advaita" means "non-dual", so we first have a division of schools of thought into dualistic and non-dualistic. Vedānta deems the non-dualistic higher than the dualistic. Vedānta is expressed in the ancient Upanishads and was primarily systematized by Shankara in the 9'th century AD. Since Vedānta prefers non-dual texts, it rejects the dualistic, theistic, aspect of the Bhagavad Gītā, and relies instead on terse texts like the Brahma-sūtras. Vedānta was popularized by the great modern sage Ramana Maharshi and via him has inspired many seekers and teachers in the West. The many contemporary neo-Advaita teachers in the west claim to be inspired by Vedānta, so let us discuss its teachings.

Brahman
Vedānta is mainly concerned with the realization of Brahman. Brahman is not an "It" or a "He" or "God", Brahman is pure being itself; the Absolute. Vedānta has some problems informing

59

us what Brahman is, since Brahman is the primal source prior to anything and thus impossible to describe. The Upanishads say that the best way of explaining what Brahman is, is by applying the expression "neti, neti" which means "not this, not this". However, we are also informed that Brahman is "sat-chit-ānanda", meaning "being-consciousness-bliss". We cannot apply "neti-neti" to being, since that would deny the existence of Brahman, nor apply it to consciousness since it would in that case be impossible to realize Brahman (Brahman would be a state of unconsciousness). Bliss has been much debated. Some maintain it is not a quality of Brahman, but rather a quality of man's apprehension of Brahman. Others maintain, correctly, that bliss is the very nature of Brahman, like being and consciousness. The difference is important: In the first case, apprehension, bliss would be seen as something that had to be overcome, in the second case, the very nature of Brahman, bliss is seen as a guide to deeper Oneness with Brahman. "Being" ("sat") is to be understood in its most ultimate sense. It is Pure Being, unqualified by anything. This means all thoughts, emotions and identities are to be transcended before one can merge with Brahman - or that all such will be transcended upon merging. "Consciousness" thus means not awareness of anything, but rather Self-awareness of itself as unmanifest, blissful being. One can speculate much along these lines, but the important thing about Vedānta is that it is not a speculative system, but is an attempt at documenting a state of enlightenment, which is considered the highest by Vedāntins.

However, Vedānta speaks of nirguna Brahman and saguna Brahman, which means Brahman without form and with form. How can Brahman have form? It cannot and the saguna Brahman refers to the inferior experience while meditating. Thus saguna Brahman is a subjective interpretation of the absolute Brahman in relative understanding. Here we have the notion of the Divine in a personal sense and saguna Brahman gives rise to devotion to, and love of, the Divine. Saguna Brahman is experienced in savikalpa samādhi (samādhi with form), while nirguna Brahman is experienced in nirvikalpa samādhi (samādhi without form). One cannot, strictly, speak of an experience in nirvikalpa samādhi; it is truly a state of pure being.

What is the relation between Brahman and the world? Vedānta has a problem here. The Upanishads give various answers, mostly relying on another philosophical system: Sāmkhya. But the general idea is that Brahman is "one without a second", in other words, Brahman transcends everything including self, God and creation. This does not answer the question of creation, though. Vedānta gives various answers, but generally maintains that the effect (the objects of creation) pre-exists as a cause within Brahman. But Brahman then becomes Īshvarā (God) which is inconsistent with the teaching "neti, neti", not this, not this. Vedānta also tries to circumvent the problem by bringing in the three concepts: māyā (illusion), avidyā (ignorance) and adhyasa (superimposition). Let us consider māyā.

Māyā

Māyā is commonly translated "illusion", but it is more complex than that. Though everything is Brahman, Brahman appears as something given, for example a pot, because of māyā. Māyā has hold over one because of one's ignorance about Brahman and because māyā superimposes the pot, for example, onto Brahman in one's consciousness. Vedānta explains it is like mistaking a rope for a snake. But Vedānta has still not solved the problem, for where does this mysterious force, māyā, come from? What drives it? What upholds it?

Whenever there is a sense of "I", "me" or "mine", there is māyā. Māyā is any kind of experience based on a subject-object relationship, it is whenever one perceives something as other than Brahman. This means identities, memories, fears, pleasures, etc. are māyā. In fact everything is māyā except the crystal-clear oneness with Brahman in unity consciousness. Since māyā as such precedes everything, it is indescribable, for language is of māyā, and māyā is unthinkable, since thoughts are of māyā. Māyā is that mysterious force which makes us take the world as real. But where does māyā come from? Māyā cannot be Brahman, since that would negate the "neti, neti" definition of Brahman. Also Brahman is a passive state of witnessing; it does not, according to Vedānta, take part in creation, since that part is played by māyā. Thus Vedānta, which claims to be non-dualistic, is in fact dualistic since it proposes two basic things:

1. A state of stasis (Brahman) untouched by māyā.

2. A dynamic creative force (māyā), hiding Brahman from Brahman and creating the world.

Ignorance (avidyā) becomes synonymous with māyā, since avidyā is non-cognition of Brahman and identification with body/ego/etc. It may be said that māyā comes from Īshvarā (God), but then the question is: how does passive Brahman become active Īshvarā? Then we have two, if not three basic principles: Brahman and Īshvarā (and māyā) and Vedānta is still a dualistic system now based in the impersonal passive divine Brahman and the personal divine Īshvarā.

Shankara explains that the world may be considered the sport or play (līlā) of Īshvarā and that it has no purpose. He also explains the world may be seen as the expansion of Īshvarā. What is not explained in Vedānta is how Īshvarā arises from passive Brahman. Vedānta tries to avoid this dilemma by insisting everything is illusion, māyā, and if everything is illusion, the dilemma is also illusion so there is no need to answer it. But this denial does not solve the problem that if Brahman is passive pure being without any causal power, how does causal power come into play as Īshvarā? This causal power may be either inherent in a super-being (Īshvarā) or may be an illusion (māyā), but nevertheless, the world is here and it is a dynamic functioning organism. So how does this dynamic functioning come about if the world is an illusion and in reality is passive Brahman?

Vedānta admits Īshvarā cannot be demonstrated rationally, but only be affirmed on the grounds of experience. So Vedānta is forced to admit there are two principles at work: Passive Brahman, and something else that has something to do with Īshvarā. (This "something else" is of course Shakti, as explained by Kashmir Shaivism. The existence of Shakti does not make a system dualistic, because the absolute in its nature is both Shiva and Shakti at once: pure being and creative energy as One.)

Vedānta maintains there is no causal relationship between Brahman and the world, that the world is the play of Īshvarā. It also maintains the world is a mere appearance of Brahman through superimposition and māyā. Thus Brahman experiences Brahman as a superimposition and is ignorant of itself believing the superimposition to be real. How does this split in Brahman come about? Vedānta has no explanation. Neither an answer to how this split is overcome. (Both can only be explained by recourse to the Kashmir Shaivism concept of Shakti.)

The Self and the self
The Self (paramātman, or just ātman) is not different from Brahman. Why then, do we think otherwise? How do we overcome ignorance of this, our very own pure being? Vedānta

relies heavily on jnāna yoga (the path of knowledge) to help set man free from ignorance. But why are we ignorant of our Self? Vedānta offers two explanations: pratibimba-vada (the theory of reflection) and avaccheda-vada (theory of limitation).

The pratibimba theory maintains the jīva (the small ignorant self) is a reflection of the Ātman (the real Self) but the reflection can be more or less pure. It is reflected in ignorance, so one has to remove ignorance to get a better reflection. Ultimately the reflection must vanish, or unite with the source. Practice is to clear the mind and calm it. One should remove desires and calm the emotions.

The aveccheda theory maintains the jīva is a limitation of pure consciousness. It rejects the theory of reflection on the basis that pure being without qualities cannot be reflected. The limitations are made up of ignorance, thus the infinite is seen through ideas and concepts that do not match the infinite. One has to clear up one's understanding.

There are five sheaths that cover the Self and with which one identifies. One has to remove identification with all of them. There is nothing wrong with this.

Annamāyākosa is one's identity as a physical body.

Prānamāyākosa is one's identity as a living, vital being.

Manomāyākosa is made up of manas, the "sense-mind" without any discriminating abilities. It gives rise to the sense of "my" and "mine" because it is manas that enables one to handle external objects.

Vijnanamāyākosa is one's identity as a thinking, rational being. It is made up of buddhi, the intellect.

Ānandamāyākosa is one's identity in deep sleep, in which one, according to Vedānta, lies in a state of bliss. This is also referred to as the causal body.

The identifications give rise to various states of consciousness. When one identifies with ānandamāyākosa, one is in deep sleep. When identified with the prāna-, mano- and vijnanamāyākosa, one is in the dream state. When identified with the physical body, one is in the waking state. Of course manas and buddhi are active in the waking state also, so one should not take this simplistic model too literally. What is interesting and important is the fourth state of consciousness, which is transcendental consciousness, or *turyā*. In this state one is temporarily free of identifications and more or less resides in the Self. By repeatedly entering turyā one will achieve Self-realization in due time. Oneness with the Self is called "samādhi"; however there are two kinds of samādhi: savikalpa and nirvikalpa. Savikalpa is imperfect while nirvikalpa is perfect, though still temporary. In savikalpa there are still mental and emotional movements, though one's awareness is sunk deeply into the Self. But it is as if only part of one's awareness is in the Self, while another part is attempting to let go of the psycho-physical movements. These movements are not directly disturbing one's samādhi, but they are never the less there. In nirvikalpa samādhi, there are no involvements with the psycho-physical movements (if there are any left) and one's entire awareness is merged with the Self. With repeated nirvikalpa samādhi one will reach Self-realization and full enlightenment.

Karma and Moksha (Liberation)

"Karma" literally means "action", but refers to a general theory that every action has an effect that one is bound to suffer, be it good or bad. It is both: *as you sow, you shall reap*, and: *as you sow, you shall act*. Vedānta, and Indian philosophy in general, does not explain karma very well and it appears to be more a convenient theory than an examined fact. Unlike the Self and samādhi, which everyone can explore and find, karma has to be intuited or taken on faith. Also you have to understand past lives in order to understand karma, for one's present life karma is to a large extent generated in past lives. The possible problem of fatalism that follows in the wake of the karma theory is obvious, but free will and responsibility for one's actions is acknowledged, though not discussed well. One could object to the karma theory, that if it was all that accounted for one's situation in life and actions, then it negated itself by denying freedom to man. But self-determinism is a given fact in Indian philosophy that is taken for granted. Karma may give one an impulse to act in some way, but it is one's own decision to decide if one wants to act thus or not. Thus the karma theory acts as a moral imperative, rather than the opposite which would follow from fatalism.

Naturally the question arises: can one be free of the effects of karma? The answer is yes and this freedom is called "moksha". Moksha is actually freedom from "bondage" and karma is the major bondage in one's life. One is also bound by one's ideas, concepts, feelings, etc. as well as the cycle of birth, death and rebirth. Moksha, however, is not solely negatively defined, it is actually more a positive concept about the attainment of Self-realization. But since Self-realization cannot be defined or described (it is only described as *neti neti*), it is common to approach it negatively. This means it is freedom from ignorance (avidyā), which in its own convoluted way says Self-realization is freedom from non-Self-realization. However, freedom is oneness with being-consciousness-bliss: Ātman, the Self, Brahman.

In order to attain moksha, one has to examine everything circumvented by the question "who am I?" This means rejecting everything conceivable and reaching the pure being prior to I-ness (ahamkāra). This kind of meditation is known as "self-enquiry" in neo-Advaita. Traditionally it is a form of jnāna-yoga, the yoga of wisdom. First one has to hear about enlightenment and moksha and so forth; then one has to think it over thoroughly. Finally one has to meditate constantly on "who am I?" rejecting all false identifications and hoping somehow to plop into savikalpa samādhi or nirvikalpa samādhi. Michael Langford refined the self-enquiry method to a question of awareness watching awareness, so that awareness would fold back in on itself and plop into samādhi. (Of course, compared to shaktipāt sādhana this self-enquiry method is incredibly slow.)

Valid Means of Knowledge

Vedānta acknowledges six valid means of knowledge: Perception, comparison, non-cognition, inference, postulation and testimony. It is noteworthy none of these methods are capable of grasping Brahman, thus Vedānta implicitly states that Brahman must be grasped by no-means. It is also noteworthy that karma can't be grasped by any of these six means and thus must be taken on faith.

Kashmir Shaivism: The Solution to Advaita Vedānta's Errors

Shaiva philosophy recognizes that the absolute is self-luminous pure being, but it solves the predicaments of Vedānta by maintaining that the absolute is not only pure being (Shiva), but that this pure being is also and simultaneously creative energy (Shakti). From one point of view the absolute is Shiva, from another point of view it is Shakti. Shiva and Shakti are one; they are not a polarity like man and woman, but are one and the same. Shakti without Shiva is unthinkable and so is Shiva without Shakti. The absolute's essential nature is consciousness and bliss. It expresses itself in will, knowledge and activity. Since it is the absolute Shiva-Shakti that itself appears in the form of subjects and objects, these appearances cannot be false. Supreme Shakti, also called Parashakti, expresses itself as the power of self-revelation (chit) and bliss (ānanda). The chit aspect of the absolute is also known as Shiva and the bliss aspect of the absolute is known as Shakti. Shakti polarizes consciousness into "I" and "this" by manifesting as the primal I-ness; however there never occurs a duality between Shiva and Shakti. Shaiva philosophy recognizes māyā and that it conceals the real nature of everything as Shiva-Shakti. Māyā is the forgetfulness of one's real nature and the real nature of things. Concealment is considered an inherent ability or function of Shiva-Shakti, just as revelation or grace is. Māyāshakti limits the power of knowledge of the individual and the individual is reduced from I AM to an individual sentient being (purusha). In each individual there is kundalinī, which is a form of Shakti, and kundalinī is nothing but the contraction of Shakti that has formed the individual sentient being (purusha) with all its limitations. Thus kundalinī also contains the key to undo the individual beings limitations and take the individual back to full recognition of Shiva-Shakti. The grace that initiates this reversal of kundalinī's binding function is

70

shaktipāt. Shaktipāt reverses the flow of kundalinī so it begins to undo limitations and reveal Shiva-Shakti in and of itself.

The Ātma Bodha by Shankara. An Advaita Vedānta Text

Shankara, called Shankarāchārya, was probably born in AD 788. He is the leading exponent of modern Advaita Vedānta.

1. This treatise about the Self is for those who are free of sin and full of peace; it is for those who are free from passions and desirous of liberation.

Some translators translate this verse so that the treatise is intended only for ascetics, as if Shankara meant that knowledge of the Self is possible for ascetics only. From a tantric perspective, anyone can desire liberation, no matter if they have practiced austerities or not. And Self-realization is not a reward for austerities, nor are austerities required to reach it. And anyone can reach liberation, no matter whether they have purified themselves or not. It is true that a certain peace and calm is required to do practices for diving into the Absolute. But on the other hand it is true that the Absolute is prior to, and undisturbed of, agitation and a troubled heart. No one can be free of cravings, since cravings are a result of the body taking care of itself, but you can merge awareness with the Self, which is prior to cravings, and ultimately this is Self-realization. So it is strange if Shankara should mean that freedom from cravings is a prerequisite for Self-realization, since such freedom only comes after Self-realization. It is likely that what is meant in this rather old-school description is the characteristics of a good student within the monastic tradition of Shankarāchārya and his time. However, it also points to the fact that people who are in complete identification with the mind and body, who are agitated and who live their life solely for gratification, are probably not going to get much from this text and will also have a harder time reaching Self-realization. Shankarāchārya answers all this in the next verse.

2. Compared to other methods, knowledge is the only means of liberation; just as cooking cannot be accomplished without fire. There is no liberation without knowledge.

Shankara answers the doubts that arouse from his first verse and makes it clear that doing austerities for purification, etc., is not the way to Self-realization. The only direct means to Self-realization is to acquire knowledge of the Self. Now, since the Self is prior to consciousness, any second hand knowledge of the Self will be wrong knowledge, therefore the only direct means to Self-realization is to practice merging with the Self repeatedly. We note Shankara's ignorance of Shakti, kundalinī and shaktipāt.

3. Because they are not mutually contradictory action cannot eliminate ignorance. Only knowledge destroys ignorance just as darkness is dispelled by light.

This verse underscores the previous verse and explains why any form of discipline cannot lead to Self-realization. The reason is that any discipline is a form of action and action is not within the nature of the Self in the same way as knowledge is. Thus the only means to Self-realization is to bring awareness out of the field of action and into that pure being prior to the I that acts. This pure being is the Self. The means to Self-realization is knowledge of the Self and knowledge of the Self is only acquired by repeatedly stepping out of the field of action (doing) and into oneness with the Self (Being). We note the absence of grace as a factor.

4. Out of ignorance the Self appears divided. When that ignorance is gone the Self shines forth just as the sun shines when the clouds are dispelled.

Ignorance is basically of the nature of confusing non-Self with Self. Since this confusion can acquire an infinite number of variations, one can never gain Self-realization by trying to remove, or purify, non-Self. Such an attempt will go on forever and never reach the Self. Shankara makes it clear once more that Self-realization is acquired by the Self revealing itself by itself.

This is the same as what is meant when stating that Self-realization is acquired through knowledge of the Self gained by merging awareness with the Self repeatedly. It makes no difference if you say awareness merges with Self, or Self reveals itself by swallowing up awareness. It is the same.

5. The soul (jivātman), infected with ignorance, is purified by the application of knowledge. After having achieved purity, knowledge itself disappears, just as the ground kataka-nut settles down in water after purifying it.

This verse refers to the small self, for the Self is not in need of purification, nor is the Self stained. Awareness is caught in a self-referential field of thoughts, emotions, experiences and desires, generating a personality, a small self. Awareness then commits the fallacy of identifying itself with this complex, or in other words: of confusing non-Self with Self. Initially practice of any kind will be within this sphere of non-Self, but when awareness merges with Self, awareness becomes free of false identifications and acquires knowledge of the Self by being the Self. Of course, knowledge of the Self does not consist in acquiring data. It is a matter of awareness first becoming aware of itself, then of awareness and Self collapsing into One Pure Being free of all identification-structures. With repeated oneness of Self and awareness, the identification-structures gradually break down. This break down is called "purification". In reality there is nothing to purify and there is no dirt to remove. There is only confusion of Self with non-Self and innumerable identifications.

6. The worldly cycle of life and reincarnation is indeed like a dream. It is full of contradictions such as desire and aversion. It appears real as long as the dream lasts, but appears unreal in the awakened state.

7. As long as the world appears true it is like believing the shine of the oyster shell is silver. This goes on as long as Brahman, the substratum of all, is not known.

In both these verses Shankara describes the difference in how the world, the mind and the I are understood before and after Self-realization. The analogy to dream and awake is not as good as it seems, because when awakening the dream goes away, however, when achieving Self-realization, the world does not go away. Self-realization is actually not awakening from a dream, even in a metaphorical sense, it is realizing who you are and have always been prior to anything in consciousness. This means that Self-realization is independent of consciousness and also that consciousness will remain largely unchanged after Self-realization. So will the world. However, in ignorance one lives in a realm of false identification and believes the identifications to be real. After Self-realization one becomes free from identifications and sees the identities as unreal. In this sense, Self-realization is an awakening from a dream that one took to be real while ignorant. Where the allegory is right on target is that before Self-realization, one believed the I AM-ness to be real, after Self-realization I-ness and I AM-ness are clearly understood to be the primal illusions separating awareness from Self. In Self-realization awareness has merged with Self, and now I-ness and I AM-ness are looked upon from the pure being prior to them. In fact, I-ness goes away. In this situation the identity, ego, mind, feelings, souls, etc. are no longer seen as the truth about oneself, and in that sense a dream has ended.

8. The pure being and consciousness of Ātman are forever sewn together. All multifarious creatures are made in and of Vishnu just as bracelets are made of gold.

Ātman: the Self.

Vishnu: While Vishnu is a personified god, Vishnu here means the all-pervading aspect of the absolute, Brahman.

9. Just as the all-pervading space is different from the various forms, so [Ātman] is different from the various forms. If the forms disappear, Ātman remains.

10. Due to association even various coatings like caste, family and social status, etc., are superimposed on the Ātman; just like taste and color is superimposed on water, and like grease floats on water.

11. The dense body composed of the five elements is the result of actions in past lives. It is the place where pleasure and pain is encountered.

12. The subtle body is the means of experience; it did not originate from the five elements but goes beyond them. It consists of 5 vital currents, 10 organs, mind and discernment.

10 organs: 5 organs of knowledge (senses) and 5 organs of action.

13. Ignorance, without beginning and indescribable, is of the causal body. One must realize that the Ātman is different from the three bodies.

I-ness (and I AM-ness) is the primal cause of all such ignorance. I-ness is prior to the "me", so is I AM-ness, yet both constitute the foundation of all ignorance. The "me" is relatively describable, but I-ness is impossible to describe. However, let's give it a try: I-ness and I AM-ness constitute the so called causal body, but in reality it is not a body as such, but a sense of being an observer or a witness, which means a subtle awareness distinct from others. It is called causal because it causes all other forms of ignorance to arise and in particular causes the sense of being an individual "me". This sense of being a "me" is the I AM-ness, and it is inseparable from I-ness. It is prior to being something, so at this level there is a sense of being nobody in particular, but just being an individual, hence it is indescribable. Yet it is not Self-realization.

14. The pure Ātman seems to borrow the qualities of the five sheaths it identifies with; just as a crystal takes on the color of blue cloth, etc. [upon which it is placed].

As soon as I AM-ness arises, there will arise a sense of being this or that; thus the pure Ātman, whose unmanifest being has contracted to the sense of "I", begins to identify with the objects of awareness. The five sheaths are:

Annamāyākosa is one's identity as a physical body.

Prānamāyākosa is one's identity as a living, vital being.

Manomāyākosa is made up of manas, the "sense-mind" without any discriminating abilities. It gives rise to the sense of "my" and "mine" because it is manas that enables one to handle external objects.

Vijnanamāyākosa is one's identity as a thinking, rational being. It is made up of buddhi, the intellect.

Ānandamāyākosa is one's identity in deep sleep, in which one, according to Vedānta, lies in a state of bliss. This is also referred to as the causal body.

15. One must separate the Ātman from the veils and destroy the connection, just as one separates the rice grain from the chaff.

Disidentification is an unavoidable and essential part of the spiritual path. One realizes more and more that one is not the personality, the body, etc. It is, however, a widely overlooked part of spiritual life.

16. Although the Ātman is omnipresent, He does not shine forth everywhere. The Ātman can only shine forth, clear as a crystal, in the discriminative awareness [buddhi].

Pure awareness can fold in on itself and realize itself as pure being, the Ātman. Though various objects in consciousness are essentially only consciousness, Ātman does not shine forth in these objects. It is only when awareness becomes aware of itself that Ātman shines forth.

17. One should realize that the Ātman, like a king, is always distinct from the body, senses, mind and intellect; all of which, along with their movements, constitute nature.

Here we are once more reminded to disidentify.

18. As the moon appears to move when the clouds move, it seems to people without discernment that the Ātman is active when the senses are active.

19. Just as men work by the light of the sun, so the actions of the body, the senses, the mind and the discriminating understanding are supported by the consciousness of the Ātman.

The Self is ever uninvolved. Yet the cognitive power that appears to belong to the mind is really supported by the Self. Thus the discriminating understanding is supported by the Self.

20. The body and the senses do the bidding of the gunas. But from lack of discernment it is ascribed to the pure being of the Ātman, just as the color blue is ascribed to the heaven.

The gunas are the three constituent dynamic principles of nature and relative consciousness (sattva, rajas and tamas). Here we are told that the Self is merely a passive witness to everything, and that it is really the gunas that cause things to happen. This is one of the problems of Vedanta: it cannot explain the connection between the relative and the absolute. This connection is explained by introducing Shakti: The relative then becomes the play of Shakti, which essentially is a play of consciousness, of the Self.

21. Just as ripples on the water may erroneously seem to be a dancing moon reflected in the water, so because of ignorance the role of doership belonging to the veils of the mind are erroneously ascribed to the Ātman.

Again we are told the Self is merely a witness to everything.

22. Attachment, desire, pleasure, pain, etc. exist as long as the discerning mind is present. They are not experienced in deep sleep when the discerning mind is not present, hence they are only of the mind and not of the Ātman.

This is not a good example. The same logic would also imply that since awareness, knowledge and bliss are not present in deep sleep, they are not essential qualities of the Self, however, they are indeed the essential qualities of the Self! Shankara remedies this flaw in the next sloka.

23. Just as luminosity belongs to the sun, coldness to water and heat to fire, so eternal and pure awareness, knowledge and bliss belong to the Ātman.

After having dealt with what the Self is not, Shankara now mentions what the Self is: awareness, knowledge and bliss.

24. The notion "I know" arises from the lack of discernment between the distinctive awareness [buddhi], the knowledge and the awareness aspect of the Ātman.

83

This is very important to understand, especially with respect to one's meditation. Here awareness has two meanings: first the distinctive mind, buddhi, then the pure awareness of the Self. Knowledge seems to lie in-between these two. The Self is neither buddhi nor the knowledge. The Self is pure awareness. The Self cannot be captured in knowledge about the Self, only by being the Self. When one merely knows something about the Self, it is surely not Self-realization but mere mind-stuff.

> **25. The Ātman never changes and is not the consciousness of the discriminating awareness [buddhi]. But the ego in us is misled into believing he is himself the seer and the knower.**

In Vedānta, the Self is understood to be totally passive. This is, however, according to Tantra only one aspect of the Self: the Shiva aspect, or the aspect of pure being. The other aspect, Shakti, is the dynamic aspect of the Self. Of course, Shakti is not part of Vedānta. In the progressively deeper and deeper levels of realization, that Shankara is taking us through, it is acceptable here to ignore Shakti and state that the Ātman is an unchanging witness to the cognitions of the discerning mind (buddhi). He is here speaking of the witnessing consciousness that arises prior to Self-realization.

26. Just as a rope can fearfully be mistaken for a snake, so the Ātman can fearfully be mistaken for the ego. But one becomes fearless again when realizing: "I am the supreme Ātman, not the individuality".

27. Just as a lamp illumines a jar, so the Ātman illumines the discriminative mind and the senses, etc. The Ātman itself is not illumined by these forms.

While the mind cannot illuminate the Self, the Self illuminates the mind. It is important to understand that the Self cannot be reached or realized through the mind.

28. Just as a lighted lamp does not need another light for its light to shine, so the Ātman, which is pure consciousness itself, does not need another consciousness to realize itself.

This is worth contemplating. The Self realizes itself by itself. Nothing is needed.

29. When, by the process of applying the scriptural statement "not this, not this" all the conditionings are

negated, then realize that the individual self is one with the supreme Self; just as the great Vedas state.

This is the first pointer about what one can do to get Self-realized. First one must understand the previous verses and reject all identifications. This is also the first time Shankara takes us to the actual state of Self-realization, where, as he says, all the conditionings are negated. The method advised is to reject all identifications and this method can only lead to first the witnessing state and second to plain Self-realization. In other words, only to the void kind of realization, which is devoid of the bliss of Shakti.

30. [Identification with] the visible world and the body, etc., arises from ignorance which is as transient as a bubble. Through discrimination you should purely realize "I am Brahman".

Ignorance is not solid, it is as transient as a bubble. Getting realized does not mean you have to change in any way; you just have to get out of illusions that are "as transient as a bubble."

31. Because I am different from the body I am free from birth, old age, weakness, death, etc. And because I am

not attached to the senses, I am free from sense impressions such as come from objects or sounds, etc.

Getting realized is not a matter of the body or something one matures into, nor is it anything that can be acquired through the senses. Again Shankara describes the witnessing kind of realization found in plain Self-realization. Only later does one begin to see the senses and the sense objects as the Self.

32. Because [I am] not the mind, I am free from sorrow, bondage, hatred and fear, etc. And I am indeed not the vital forces. It is also on authority of the sacred scriptures that [I am] radiant and not the mind.

Furthermore getting realized is not a matter of the mind, nor of the vital forces (prāna).

33. Everything is born: the vital breaths, the mind, the senses, as well as ether, air, light, water, earth and all that upholds existence.

In fact getting realized has nothing to do with vital breaths or the elements that uphold existence.

34. I am without attributes, without action, eternal, without mind fluctuations, spotless, changeless, formless, forever liberated and pure.

First one should realize that the Self is absolutely nothing, it is void. There is no movement in the Self and it has no plurality what so ever.

35. Like space itself, I fill all things within and without. I am always the same in everything; perfect, unbound, pure and motionless.

The Self, being unmanifest, can be said to be omnipresent. Though this is strictly not true, since omnipresence would demand spatiality, and there is no such spatiality in the Self. Nevertheless, Shankara is now moving on to a higher level of realization, known as unity consciousness. In unity consciousness one realizes that the unmanifest Self underlies everything.

The Tripura Rahasya says of this state: "Unless a man live in the ordinary life and check every incident as the projection of the Self, not swerving from the Self in any circumstances, he cannot be said to be free from the handicap of ignorance." (XVII, 109).

36. I am indeed that transcendental Brahman which is eternal, pure, free, singular and indivisible; which is non-dual and infinite truth and knowledge.

After having studied what the Self is not, we are presented with some of the qualities of the Self.

37. Indeed, the constant awareness of "I am Brahman" takes away ignorance and mind fluctuations just as medicine cures diseases.

This is the second instruction: Now one should understand one's true identity, which is oneness with Brahman (the absolute). This is the means to move from plain Self-realization to unity consciousness. Merely repeating to oneself "I am Brahman" is not what is being advocated. One has to be that oneness.

38. Sit in a lonely place, free of passions and with controlled senses, and meditate one-pointedly on the Ātman, which is infinite and singular.

This is the third instruction: One should meditate one-pointedly on the Self.

39. Indeed one should meditate wholly on the Ātman with a completely dissolved mind. Always see the Ātman as spotless as the ether [ākāsha].

This is the fourth instruction: The correct way to meditate on the Self, according to Vedanta, is with no-mind. If one meditates with or within the mind, one will not reach the Self. Only when the mind is transcended can one realize the Self. Again we note the lack of understanding of Shakti.

40. When one has realized the Ātman, form, color, etc. [falls off]. Then one knows the highest goal and lives as an embodiment of perfect consciousness and bliss.

Up until now we have been instructed to meditate on the Self. What, then, is it like to realize the Self? It is utter freedom from any qualification. Furthermore it is pure, unmanifest consciousness and bliss.

41. In the supreme Ātman, there are no such distinctions as the knower, the knowing and the known. One has realized pure being and bliss. That [realization] shines by itself from oneself.

This is important to understand. One's small self has fallen away; or rather there is no longer any identification with it.

42. When, from constant meditation on the joyous Self, the fire of knowledge is born, it burns up all ignorance as if it were fuel.

Now we are introduced to the essence of Vedāntic meditation: It is an often repeated diving into the joyous Self that dispels all ignorance. In sloka 29 rejection of identification (*neti, neti*) was the means. This is not a contradiction, as it may seem, but rather two sides of the same coin. One does not become realized simply by rejecting everything; one also has to dive into the Self again and again.

43. As darkness is dispelled by the sun at dawn, so ignorance is removed when the Ātman emerges.

There are layers of ignorance, but not until the time when the Self emerges will root-ignorance be removed.

44. The Ātman is always present, however this is not realized because of ignorance. When ignorance is

destroyed one becomes radiant like a [shining] chain around one's neck.

What, then, is getting realized like? It is an interesting paradox that the Self is always present and one is really already realized; only one does not know it. Getting realized is getting rid of what one does not have (ignorance).

45. As one during a walk may erroneously mistake a tree stump for a man, so one may mistake the individual soul for Brahman; this error disappears when the true nature of the individual soul is realized.

Furthermore, when realized, one no longer misidentifies the Self with anything else, as one did before.

46. Just as one gone astray [may return to the right path with right knowledge], so the ignorance of "I", "me" and "mine" is quickly dispelled with right knowledge.

47. The yogi of perfect realization sees the whole universe as the Self. He considers everything to be the Self in absolute wisdom.

Shankara now speaks of perfect realization, implying there are imperfect kinds of realization. Indeed the void-consciousness of plain Self-realization is imperfect realization compared to unity consciousness.

48. This world is verily the Ātman, everything is Ātman and nothing is different from Ātman. Similarly pots are made of clay and remain clay despite being pots. Thus the wise sees everything as himself.

This is the state of unity consciousness. Up to verse 37 Shankara has been talking about Self-realization, and in verse 37 to 46 about how one moves on to unity consciousness, now he talks about the state of unity consciousness.

49. He is liberated while alive and is one who knows "That", and has removed the veils of the gunas; he is filled up with existence, consciousness and bliss. It is similar to a caterpillar becoming a butterfly.

50. After having crossed the ocean of delusion and having slain passion and hatred, etc., the yogi dwells in peace and radiates the joy of the Self.

51. [The yogi] who abides in his Self, who is detached from fluctuating pleasures, is unmoved in the happiness of the Ātman. He is like a light placed inside a pot: He shines inwardly.

52. Though the wise one lives within the conditionings he is detached as the clear sky and may behave like a fool, though he is all-knowing. He is as unbound as the wind.

There are no outward signs that tell if a person is realized or not.

53. Upon the destruction of the conditionings, the wise one is completely absorbed in Vishnu. Like water in water, air in air and fire in fire.

"Vishnu" here means the all-pervading aspect of the absolute, not the personified god.

54. With that accomplished there is nothing left to achieve. With that happiness, there is nothing more to enjoy. With that knowledge, there is nothing more to know. One must understand that is Brahman.

55. When having seen that, one need see no more. When having become that, one need not be reborn. When knowing that, one need know no more. That is Brahman and is what one must realize.

56. Realize that to be Brahman which is crosswise, up, down and full, which is existence-consciousness-bliss, and which is undivided, infinite, eternal and one.

"Crosswise, up, down and full": Omnipresent.

57. Realize that to be Brahman which is found by the Vedantic method of rejection and negation, which is non-dual, indivisible, blissful and One.

58. Though bliss is indivisible, Brahma and other gods enjoy a mere fraction of the supreme bliss in various degrees.

59. All objects are pervaded by Brahman, all activities are pervaded by Brahman; thus Brahman permeates everything as butter permeates milk.

60. Realize that to be Brahman which is neither fine nor coarse; neither short nor long; without birth or change; formless, colorless and without qualities.

61. Realize that to be Brahman which shines like the sun that illumines everything, but which is not illumined by anything.

62. Brahman pervades the whole world within and without with its luminance, like a glowing ball of iron in the fire.

63. Brahman is different from the world, yet there exists nothing that is not Brahman. Out of ignorance something else may seem to exist, like a mirage.

64. Whatever is seen or heard is Brahman and nothing else. Viewed from the knowledge of truth, everything is Brahman: Non-dual existence-knowledge-bliss.

65. The omnipresent Ātman which is existence and consciousness is only seen through the eye of wisdom. Anyone who looks through the eye of ignorance sees nothing, like the blind man sees not the sun.

66. Clarified by hearing etc., lit in the fire of knowledge, the soul is freed from all evil and shines of itself like gold.

67. Indeed the Ātman, having risen in the space of the heart like the sun of wisdom, removes all ignorance like the sun dispels darkness. Its shine is all-pervasive and all supportive and it makes everything glow.

Having just been informed Ātman is omnipresent, it is strange we are now informed Ātman arises in the heart. "Heart" is probably to be understood as a metaphor for the essential pure Being.

68. He who gives up all activities, who worships the omnipresent Self in itself, who is not bound by time, place or direction, he enjoys eternal happiness and is free from confusion, cold, etc., he is omniscient, all-pervading and has finally achieved immortality.

THUS CONCLUDES THE ĀTMA-BODHA.

Highlights from the Tripura Rahasya

Tripura Rahasya is an ancient Sanskrit text. It is quite extensive, so I have picked out the essential teachings on Self-realization and added commentaries. Tripura Rahasya is a significant Tantra text. Literally "Tripura" means "three cities", but refers to the three common states of consciousness: wakefulness, dream and deep sleep. The underlying fourth state is turyā and is here called Devi or Shakti. But the text itself makes it clear that the one reality behind everything has many names:

> **The whole universe is thus in the illumination which shines self-sufficient, by itself, everywhere, and at all times. Such illumination is Her Transcendental Majesty Tripura, the Supreme. She is called Brahmā in the Vedas, Vishnu by the Vaishnavites, Siva by the Shaivaites, and Shakti by the Shaktas. There is indeed nothing but She. (XIV: 43-45)**

Tripura Rahasya is an essential book on Advaita Vedānta. Much praised by Ramana Maharshi. But it is certainly also a Shakta text. I read it first and foremost from the Shakta perspective. One will find that the highest teachings of Vedānta are largely in agreement with the highest teachings of the Shakta viewpoint -

with the exception that the Shakta viewpoint incorporates divine Grace from the divine Mother: Mother's grace or Shakti as it is known. The path of Vedānta is a dull and dry bone in comparison to the Tantra of kundalinī shaktipāt yoga.

The text and commentaries:

> **Investigation is the root-cause of all, and it is the first step to the supreme reward of indescribable bliss. How can anyone gain security without proper investigation? (II: 51-52)**

Without investigating the teachings about supreme bliss, one will not take even the first step towards Self-realization and one will stay deluded. What is investigation? It means contemplating the teachings and also practicing enquiry into the subject of the teachings - being the Self. Thus one should practice Self-enquiry along with reflecting on the teachings. Ask yourself: Who am I? The question in itself won't take you to the Self, but without interest in that basic question, the whole idea of sādhana for Self-realization becomes kind of pointless.

> **Investigation is analysis conducted within oneself, discriminating the non-Self from the Self, stimulated by**

99

a stern, strong and sincere desire to realize the Self. (XXI: 95)

Investigation is the Sun for chasing away the dense darkness of indolence. It is generated by the worship of God with devotion. When the supreme Devi is well pleased with the worship of the Devotee, She turns into vichāra [discrimination] in him and shines as the blazing Sun in the expanse of the Heart. (II: 69-70)

Worship of God with devotion does not mean formal ritualistic worship, but inner surrender. Surrendering to Devi (Shakti, the Divine Mother) is part of the investigation. It is not enough to simply ponder the teachings mentally, one should also surrender to the essence of the teachings and experience them for oneself. Upon merging with Devi, one's understanding of the teachings change at once. This is what is meant with the phrase that "Devi is well pleased" and "She turns into vichāra". Vichāra means discrimination, investigation, judgment. So proper understanding of the texts and teachings is only acquired by Mother's grace. Investigation with devotional surrender is, however, the first step one should take on the path to Self-realization. One should gain not only a mental understanding of the teachings, but also gain Mother's grace through surrendering to her internally. Internal surrender to Mother's grace, means surrendering to the Shakti within (kundalinī). Kundalinī-shakti needs to awaken; then grace flows abundantly.

I shall now tell you the fundamental cause of salvation. Association with the wise is the root cause for obliterating all misery. (III: 7)

Such will lead to "a stage of enlightenment, which is the fore-runner of emancipation." (III: 8-9). This is very interesting. Association with the wise is contagious, so to speak. This phenomenon is known as shaktipāt. The benefit of association with the wise cannot be mere theoretical knowledge, for that is what is gained by the kind of investigation mentioned previously, or is what can be gained from books. It is the mere association with the wise, not studying with the wise or learning from them, but merely being in their company; hanging out with them. This association will automatically lead Shakti to jump from the wise one to the devoted student. Once the Shakti is ignited in the student, Mother's grace will begin to flow and vichāra will come automatically. This is divine grace and it is shaktipāt.

One of the things that will grow with vichāra is dispassion and displeasure with worldly things. In other words, misery will reveal itself to the student. Vichāra can go along these lines:

That cannot be happiness, my Lord, which is tinged with misery. Misery is of two kinds: external and internal. The former pertain to the body and is caused by the nerves, etc., the latter pertains to the mind and is caused by desire. (IV: 19-20)

In other words, some types of misery are neurological, others are psychological. The psychological are worse than the neurological (with regard to getting Self-realized) since they are "the seed of the tree of misery and never fails on its fruits." (IV: 21). Physical and neurological misery may be unbearable, but they are not sources of bondage. Psychological misery, on the other hand, causes bondage by being tied into the cycle of desire-gain-loss-suffering-desire-etc. Even during the happiness when one's desire has been fulfilled, there is the seed of more desire, so the happiness is doomed to fail and go away. Only the happiness found in the Self is everlasting. One must surrender to Mother's grace and associate with the wise.

After scrutinizing the misery of the ignorant state and surrendering to Mother's grace, one may reach liberation:

Then realizing the pure consciousness inhering in the Self to be that self-same Tripura, he became aware of the One Self holding all, and was liberated. (IV: 94).

Tripura is the Supreme Goddess, Devi, Shakti. She has many names, but is essentially the Divine Mother and grace. One has to realize one's oneness with Mother. The text summarizes:

That same consciousness is also the objects, that is the subject, and that is all – the mobile and the immobile; all else shines in its reflected light; it shines of itself. Therefore, O Man, throw off delusion! Think of that consciousness which is alone, illuminating all and pervading all. (IV: 100-101)

Association with the sages, O Rama, is thus the root cause of all that is auspicious and good. (IV: 104)

In the high state of enlightenment, unity consciousness, one will realize that Shakti is not only internal, but external also. Everything is one pure consciousness, illuminating all and pervading all. Again we are informed that association with the wise is the basic means to liberation.

On the path to enlightenment, dispassion will arise and one will find that objects and events, that used to please one, have become dull and meaningless.

This state of dispassion only arises in one with whose continued devotion Tripura, inherent in the Heart as the Self, is well pleased. (V: 28)

Mother resides in everybody's "heart" as the Self. "Heart" is a metaphor for one's innermost being. Only when Self-realization begins to flower, will dispassion arise. Compared to the bliss of the Self, everything else fades into insignificance. This can be annoying and frustrating, since one is not yet Self-realized and the bliss therefore only arises in fleeting samādhis. Nevertheless, the dispassion is productive with respect to getting enlightened. It quiets the mind and the passions, so one becomes more focused on getting enlightened. One will seek out people who can help on the path, but the Tripura Rahasya warns us:

He who is bent on the highest good should never trust an incompetent person. Otherwise he comes to grief ... (VI: 34)

What makes a person competent, or qualified, to aid one in this difficult phase? Only one who is Self-realized himself. There are many teachers of spirituality, yoga and meditation, but they are not to be considered competent teachers if they are not Self-realized. The most competent teacher not only is Self-realized, but gives shaktipāt initiation. Otherwise they are merely teaching a system and a method, which one will get stuck in. Blind acceptance leads nowhere, similarly endless discussions lead nowhere. Too much faith in a system or a method leads only to expert performance of the method, not to eternal bliss. Purposeful discussion is of course appropriate, but it should never be considered the end in itself.

Appropriate effort must follow right discussion. (VII: 7)

Appropriate effort is of course to meditate with surrender to the Self. However, even the desire to possess an appropriate method is born of delusion (VII: 24). This complicates the matter. One should not be attached to the method one uses, but be prepared to let it go at the appropriate moment - which is when one sees the Self, or feels the Self as bliss. When bliss comes, one surrenders to the bliss and lets one's full attention be filled with the bliss. Bliss is of the Self, so it is a safe guide to follow. It is pure grace when bliss grabs you, it means kundalinī shakti has grabbed you and will guide you home.

Men can learn to overcome the universal Māyā if only the Lord is gracious to them, they can never escape from Māyā, without His grace. (VII: 29)

Māyā is the great illusion keeping people in ignorance about the Self. Without grace it is impossible to reach the Self. Who is the Lord? It is ultimately the Self. The grace of the Self comes as Shakti. Shakti resides within you as kundalinī. By the grace of Mother Shakti, kundalinī awakens and you experience the bliss of the Self quickly. The concentrated form of grace that awakens kundalinī is known as shaktipāt. One should worship Mother by doing practices to awaken and arouse kundalinī. They should be done with loving devotion to Mother and gratitude for Her grace.

> **Other methods are also put forward as serving this supreme end, but they are bound to fail in their purpose if the Lord's grace be not forthcoming. Therefore worship the Primal Cause of the universe as the starting point; be devoted to Him; He will soon enable you to succeed on your attempts to destroy the illusion. (VII: 32-33)**

Why is the Lord mentioned as masculine, when we speak of Mother's grace? This is just the old patriarchal tradition. Tripura Rahasya states "You know the Mother only if you know the Self" (IX: 7) and the text simply refers to the Self as both He and She in an odd mixture. The Divine Mother and the Divine Father are One and are known as Shakti and Shiva. You cannot invoke one without invoking the other. Mother's grace gives oneness with

Shiva and Shiva's grace gives oneness with Shakti. Shiva's grace resides within you as the ever present Self; Mother's grace resides within you as the ever active kundalinī. Ultimately, kundalinī is the Self and when it is awakened it will give Self-realization as oneness with Shiva-Shakti. Similarly, the grace of Shiva will reveal the Self in its blissful purity - and this will in time awaken kundalinī so the bliss of the Self will be felt not only to be one's Self, but be felt in every cell of the body as bliss.

Surrender yourself directly and unhesitatingly to Him. He will ordain the best for you and you need not ask for it. Among the methods of approach to God, there are (1) worship to overcome troubles, (2) worship to gain wealth, etc., and (3) loving dedication of oneself. The last one is the best and the surest in its results. (VII: 50-51)

Remarkable as it sounds, it is quite true that once your kundalinī has been awakened by the grace of shaktipāt, then "He" (the Self, Shiva) "will ordain what is best for you and you need not ask for it". Spontaneously you will know how to meditate and various kriyās (spontaneous activities) will take place either internally as visions, or externally as movements of the body. However, control of breath is recommended (VII: 63) as a means to overcome one's karma.

Here is one simple method: Breathe in, hold the breath and breathe out for equal durations of time. You could count to three or four during each phase. When breathing in, sense energy rising up the spine and into the brain, when holding the breath and when breathing out, imagine energy radiating from the brain in all directions. That is one round; do as many as you like. This wonderful and simple prāṇāyāma will soon awaken kundalinī and grant you Mother's grace.

When you begin to meet the Self, you will think of it as "my Self", however, the Self is not yours, it is You. This ignorance has to be overcome. In meditation, analyze the things you think of as "mine" and discard those notions. Consider "my bliss"; no it is not your bliss, the bliss is You. "My thoughts", no the thoughts are not yours, they just happen to agitate your mind for a while. Likewise, you are not "your mind". And so on. Also get rid of external attachments, like "my body", "my spouse" etc. Finally arrest the thoughts and a blank will supersede. Think of this blank as the Self. A brilliant inner light may fill the blankness. After this, bliss may fill you. Or bliss may come before the light. In either case surrender to the bliss. First it will be ecstatic, but if you remain calm, you will transcend the ecstasy and sink into oneness with the Self as bliss. This is nirvikalpa samādhi. Remember:

It [arresting thoughts and turning inwards] does not produce Self-realization for the Self remains realized at all times. (IX: 69)

You just have to sink into the Self. Nothing has to be developed or evolved. Controlling the mind is a good beginning, but surrender is the best, and controlling the mind does not give you Self-realization.

The knower does not require any tests for knowing his own existence. The knower therefore is the only reality behind knowledge and objects. That which is self-evident without the necessity to be proved is alone real; not so other things. (IX: 88)

The knower is the Self. The Self is always there, perfect, pure, behind objects of the mind and the minds knowledge. Once realized, it is understood that the Self is self-evident. The Self reveals itself by itself, not by any method or knowledge. The Self-revelation of the Self is grace. However, with a still mind, one may find the Self at various situations:

Realize with a still mind the state between sleep and wakefulness, the interval between the recognition of one

109

**object after another or the gap between two perceptions.
(IX: 94)**

Let your mind relax and be outgoing as it will, then turn it inward, control it just a little and watch for the Self. Remember that "the investigator is himself the essence of being and the Self of Self." (IX: 98). The notion "I see" will arise, but be free of that also. The next problem is that you lose the state when you open your eyes. With a little experience of merging with the Self, you can begin to practice with open eyes and also during activity. Hold the bliss with open eyes; calmly look around and recognize that Mother's grace is omnipresent.

**That which shines as "Is" is Her Majesty the Absolute
Consciousness. Thus the universe is only the Self – the
One and only. (XI: 85)**

By force of habit, the wakeful universe appears real. Imagine it as vacuous. Fill everything with void. Realize this void to be Shakti, the Divine Mother, the Self.

**Realize that the Self is the self-contained mirror
projecting and manifesting this world. The Self is pure**

unblemished consciousness. Be quick! Realize it quickly and gain transcendental happiness! (XIII: 91)

This realization is the high enlightenment of unity consciousness. But transcendental happiness can be gained simply within. It is not necessary to also have it without in the beginning. In god-consciousness one has realized the Self to be Mother, Shakti, and one recognizes this without also. And this is bliss. It is not an experience of bliss, it is simply bliss. There is no experiencer; you simply are that bliss and that pure being which is Shakti. Why is the Absolute called by so many names and personified in so many ways? Out of love and because people are different.

The whole universe is thus in the illumination which shines self-sufficient, by itself, everywhere, and at all times. Such illumination is Her Transcendental Majesty Tripura, the Supreme. She is called Brahmā in the Vedas, Vishnu by the Vaishnavites, Siva by the Shaivaites, and Shakti by the Shaktas. There is indeed nothing but She. (XIV: 43-45)

Therefore recognize the fact that the world is simply an image on the mirror of consciousness and cultivate the contemplation of 'I am', abide as pure being and thus give up this delusion of the reality of the world. (XIV: 92)

111

The important thing is 'pure being', not 'I am'. This becomes clear next:

True experience of the Self is the unawareness of even 'I am' (XV: 26)

What does this statement mean? At first it means transcending the 'I am' state, which is very true. But it also says "unawareness of even ..." which means the experience of the Self is a state of unawareness of anything. "Unawareness" must be discussed, for otherwise it will be assumed the experience of the Self is a state of unconsciousness. The experience of the Self is concentrated awareness in its purity, it is not unconsciousness, for during the experience one is (generally) conscious of the surroundings, but internally one has merged into the innermost pure being, which is consciousness-being-bliss.

This is due to the Grace of God which puts you in the right way of investigation. Who can attain anything worthy without divine Grace? (XV: 22)

The beneficent work of the self-inhering divine Grace is finished when the inward turning of one's mind increases in strength day by day. (XV: 23)

112

This is important to understand. You can get a high or two during the course of your meditations, but they are not sure signs that Shakti has grabbed you. Only when bliss sucks you in more and more day by day, can you say Shakti has grabbed you. It will go up and down of course, but by and large Mother's Grace will more and more tingly blissfully in your entire body and pull your attention inwards into the Self. Can one know the Self in the form of knowledge gained through repeated experience? One might think so, but it is not the case:

It is also unknowable because there is no one to know it, besides itself. (XV: 62)

"No one ... besides itself"; this is important to understand. The Self knows itself; the mind knows the body's and mind's reactions to samādhi and mistakes these for the Self. As one's sādhana progresses and one gains more and more samādhis, which means more and more knowledge of the Self, one should understand that a split will arise between the knowledge as an after-effect of samādhi, and the Self's temporary Self-realization during the samādhi. Thus a split arises between the minds knowledge based on repeated experience, and the blissful pure being permeating one's awareness and body more and more. Yes: one's body: it is a very physical thing when you get grabbed by Mother's Grace (kundalinī shakti). This split is most curious:

There is mind with its self-referential knowledge assuming the status of a self, and then there is the Self's realization of itself.

> **Therefore become dispassionate and inhere as the Self. Such inherence is spontaneous. It is realized after thoughts are eliminated and investigation ceases. (XV: 85)**

Actually, you do not need to eliminate thoughts, you just have to step out of the mind, meaning out of the thoughts, and into the Self. This, of course, means an elimination of the thoughts with respect to your Self-awareness. In this state dispassion arises; one simply wants nothing more than to stay in the immense bliss of the Self. When abiding in the Self, there is no need for further investigation. Actually one has to stop investigation just prior to merging with the Self. The final plop into the Self is pure Grace; one has to let go of everything and surrender to Mother's Grace. This is what is meant with the statement that it "is spontaneous".

> **Recapitulate your state after you break off from it, and then [you] will know all and the significance of its being knowable and unknowable at the same time. Thus realizing the unknowable, one abides in immortality forever and ever. (XV: 85)**

114

It is an important part of one's sādhana to recapitulate one's samādhi states after meditation. One can simply recall the state and contemplate it for a while, or one can talk a little about it with a fellow sadhaka (spiritual seeker) one trusts and can rely on. This will help both, - if neither becomes jealous of the others experiences and insights, but rather becomes inspired. But by and large it is good to keep quiet about one's experiences and insights. One should, though, recapitulate one's samādhis for oneself. This helps the mind get a grasp on what is going on and it helps establish the peculiar split mentioned above between the minds notion of a self, and the real Self's Self-realization. Thus the unknowability of the Self for the mind becomes clear, and one realizes the unknowable by merging awareness into the Self.

This transcendental state is quite easy or may be well-nigh impossible according as one's mind is inward bent in peace or out-moving in restlessness. It cannot be taught if it always remains unknown. (XVI: 12-13)

Now we are reminded that it depends on one's state of mind whether it is easy or difficult to reach the transcendental state. If the mind is inward bent in peace, then it is quite easy. If the mind is out-moving in restlessness it is quite difficult. Thus one has to calm the mind and stay focused. The last sentence is interesting: "It cannot be taught if it always remains unknown". This means that one cannot teach the transcendental to one who has never experienced it. One has to experience it directly for oneself. Teachings can merely point in the right direction. Here is one such pointer:

Carefully watch absolute Intelligence after eliminating all else from it. (XVI: 19)

Here "absolute Intelligence" is synonymous with the pure awareness of pure being. The word "watch" implies awareness watching, and what it should watch is itself as absolute Intelligence.

Abstract Intelligence can thus be made manifest by eliminating from it all that can be known. It cannot be known as such and such, for it is the supporter of one and all. (XVI: 21)

By letting go of everything in one's awareness, abstract intelligence can be known in and of itself. There is another valid way to the Self, though: We know from experience and from other places in the text that the Self can be experienced as sat-chit-ānanda, meaning as blissful pure being. Thus bliss (ānanda) is a guide into the Self as well as abstract intelligence (chit). The

116

Self can be known as pure bliss, but this knowledge of pure bliss arises not in the mind, but in the soul as one more or less merges with the Self. This blissful merging is making the abstract intelligence manifest. It does not manifest as something concrete, what is meant is that abstract intelligence becomes self-aware. This self-awareness requires that all else is let go of, or eliminated from awareness.

Self-realization [...] requires only one condition: Elimination of all perceptions. (XVI: 33)

This is easy to misunderstand. One should not fight one's perceptions, but withdraw awareness from them. The senses will go on perceiving even while in samādhi, but awareness should be so self-absorbed that perceptions do not get any awareness at all. Thus perceptions can be said to be eliminated. In actual fact, perceptions cannot be eliminated since the perceptual apparatus will go on doing its job automatically.

But since consciousness is the Self and not apart from the mind, concentration on it is not necessary for its realization. It is enough that other perceptions should be eliminated from the mind and then the Self will be realized. (XVI: 38-39)

The point is that even though the mind cannot cognize the Self, the mind is of the Self. Similarly consciousness cannot be conscious of what the Self is, but consciousness is of the Self. This means that when consciousness is empty of content (perceptions, ideas, etc.), or when the mind is similarly empty, there is nothing left but the Self and in that state the Self can realize itself.

> **Diversion of attention from other items is all that is necessary for Self-realization. [...] consciousness of the Self becomes manifest by mere diversion of attention from things or thoughts. Realization of Self requires absolute purity only and no concentration of mind. [...] the only impurity of the mind is thought. To make it thought-free is to keep it pure. (XVI: 45-48)**

It is a relief that concentration of mind is not necessary for Self-realization. Developing concentration can take a long time. What one should practice is alertness and retraction of awareness from objects and thoughts. It is necessary to have an alert mind (XVI: 62). A stupefied mind is of no use. An interesting consequence of this observation is that people throughout the day must experience fleeting small unions with the Self when their minds happen to be alert and thought free. And so they do, but these fleeting unions go undetected because people are unaware of the Self. These fleeting unions are not to be called "samādhi" proper, because all the proclivities of the mind are still there latent and ready to manifest. So, fleeting unions are useless because they go unnoticed. If one learns to notice them, though, they will be of value (XVII: 18), but they will not in themselves lead to Self-realization (XVII: 39). For Self-realization to happen nirvikalpa samādhis are necessary. Also Mother's grace is needed:

> **Only those transcend māyā with whose devotion the Goddess of the Self is pleased: such can discern well and happily. Being by the grace of God endowed with proper discernment and right-earnestness, they become established in transcendental Oneness and become absorbed. (XVII: 61-62)**

So the necessary cocktail is devotion to the Self via Mother, Mother's grace and a still mind by pulling attention out of thoughts and things.

> **After experiencing the Inner Self, he will be able to identify the Self with the Supreme and thus destroy the root of ignorance. The inner Self is realized in advanced contemplation and that state is called nirvikalpa samādhi. Memory of that realization enables one to**

identify the Inner Self with the Universal Self. (XVII: 68-69)

Interestingly nirvikalpa samādhi is not enough. It is the "memory" of nirvikalpa samādhi that "enables one to identify the Inner Self with the Universal Self". Unity consciousness is not solely a result of nirvikalpa samādhi, but of the active part of recalling and holding the state during activity.

Unless a man live the ordinary life and check every incident as the projection of the Self, not swerving from the self in any circumstances, he cannot be said to be free from the handicap of ignorance. (XVII: 109)

This state is "sahaja" samādhi (natural samādhi). It is then in one's very nature to see the Self in everything; and one's awareness never leaves the Self with which it is united. The fact that this state is possible and desirable and that it is characterized solely by oneness with the Self, has some interesting consequences. First of all it means the Self has always been there and is already perfect; second, it means you are already the Self, you just don't know it.

Such pure mind entirely divested of all objective knowledge [or thoughts] is pure intelligence. Awareness is its nature. Therefore it is always realized, for no other knower beside itself can ever be admitted. (XVIII: 5)

Now, this has some further consequences regarding the question of moksha (freedom from ignorance, reincarnation and from karma):

Moksha is not anything to be got afresh for it is already there, only to be realized. Such realization arises with the elimination of ignorance. Absolutely nothing more is required to achieve the aim of life. (XVIII: 19)

Freedom from ignorance and a life in bliss is considered the aim of life. To reach this state nothing more is required than to eliminate ignorance. This is because the Self is already perfect and blissful; it is just covered with a layer of ignorance that has to be removed. You don't have to change to gain the Self, you only have to stop being ignorant; ignorance is only a bad habit. The bad habit is to contract and become limited when stimuli arise in the mind; otherwise the Self is infinite and unbroken (XVIII: 29). One should change the bad habit of being ignorant, to the habit of preserving the unlimited, unmanifest, infinite space of the Self, even while dealing with the world.

The greatest of all delusions is the conviction that knowledge is not a delusion. (XVIII: 156)

This is very true. As the Shiva Sutras says: "Knowledge is bondage" (I:2). Liberated people (jnānis) are not all alike. They are just as different as everybody else. Tripura Rahasya (XVIII: 162-65) divides enlightened people into three categories:

1) Jnānis of the highest order are never detached from the enjoyment of their bliss even if confronted with a million times more karma [prārabda karma]; they are not surprised at the most unnatural and miraculous happenings; they are not elated by the greatest pleasures, nor depressed by the worst miseries. They are always peaceful and calm within, although they appear to act like common folk

2) Jnānis of the higher [middle] order even while reaping the fruits of their past karma are however firmer in their natural happiness like men inebriated with drink.

3) [Jnānis of the lowest order] know the Self and yet are influenced by the pleasures and pains accruing to them according to their past karma [prārabda karma].

These differences are due to the differences in their intellects and to the degrees of development of jnāna [wisdom, enlightenment]. Their activities depend on their predispositions as determined by their past karma. (XVIII: 165-66)

So some enlightened beings live a life within the pleasures and pains of karma; other enlightened beings also do so, but are in a state of permanent bliss; yet others are entirely free of karma and also live in bliss. It is unclear at this point what kind of samādhi the lowest class of jnānis enjoy. Tripura Rahasya elaborates further:

Now the lowest order of jnānis, still under the influence of their minds, know that there is no truth in the objective universe. Their samādhis are not different from the rest. (XIX: 112)

The jnānis of the lowest order behave like ignorant men in their care for their bodies. They have not attained sahaja samādhi. They are in the state of perfection only when they are calm or composed. They have as much of the body sense and enjoy pleasure and pain with as much zest as any animal when they are not engaged in the investigation of the Self. [...] All the same, they are

emancipated because the animal-sense is only an aberration during interludes of imperfection and does not always leave any mark on them. (XXI: 38-44)

To be liberated (having attained moksha) does not require that one lives in sahaja samādhi. The lowest class of jnānis are liberated simply by their ability to enter oneness with the Self at will. They are not consciously one with the Self during much of their activity, only when they are "calm and composed" and investigate into the Self.

The middle class of jnānis are never deluded by their bodies. Delusion is the false identification of 'I' with the body. [...] The middle class of jnānis are never attached to the body. Their minds are mostly dead because of their long practice and continued austerities. They are not engaged in work because they are entirely self-possessed. [...] But he is aware of his actions. His body continues on account of his vāsanās [predispositions] and destiny. (XXI: 50-52)

Unlike the lowest class of jnānis, the middle class are constantly aware of the Self and are never caught up in karma. That "they are not engaged in work" does not mean they are lazy and don't work, it means they are so Self-possessed they do not identify with the work or the worker. "He is aware of his actions", but is disidentified from them. This class of jnānis remains steadfast through sustained practice and control of mind.

> **Jnānis of the highest class do not identify the Self with the body but remain completely detached from their bodies. Their work is like that of a charioteer driving the chariot, who never identifies himself with the chariot. Similarly the jnāni is not the body nor the actor; he is pure intelligence. Though entirely detached from action within, to the spectator he seems to be active. He performs his part like an actor in a drama; and plays with the world as a parent does with a child. (XXI: 53-54)**

The highest class of jnānis remains steadfast through the force of his discrimination and investigation. In contrast, the middle class remained so due to sustained practice. The highest jnāni is in sahaja samādhi (constant natural samādhi), whereas the middle class remains in samādhi due to habit of practice and investigation.

The lower class of jnānis:

Jnānis of the lowest order also enjoy pleasure and pain like the ignorant, but their remembrance of such experiences is frequently broken up by intervals of realization. Thus the worldly enjoyments do not leave an impression on their mind. (XXII: 37)

As for the lowest order of jnānis, these realize the Self off and on, and spells of ignorance overtake them whenever overcome by their predispositions, they look upon the body as the Self and the world as real. They are often able to over-ride the old tendencies, and thus there is a struggle between wisdom and ignorance – each of them prevailing alternatively. The jnāni ranges himself on the side of wisdom and fights against ignorance until falsity is thoroughly blown out, and truth prevails. (XXII: 43-49)

The middle class of jnānis:

Jnānis of the middle class, accustomed to controlling their minds by long-continued austerities, keep their minds in check even while enjoying pleasure and pain, and thus their response to the world is as indistinct as that of a man in sleep to a gentle breeze playing on him or an ant creeping over his body. (XXII: 38)

Forgetfulness of the Self never overtakes a middle class jnāni and wrong knowledge never possesses him. However, he of his own accord brings out some predispositions from his own depths in order to maintain his body according to prārabdha [karma active in this life]. This is the conduct of an accomplished jnāni. (XXII: 50-51)

The middle order jnāni is fond of samādhi and voluntarily abides in it. There is accordingly a lapse, however slight, when he is engaged in worldly affairs, or even in the maintenance of his body. (XXII: 54)

The highest class of jnānis:

Jnānis of the highest order are left untouched for [...] just as an actor is not really affected by the passions which he displays on the stage, so also this jnāni, always aware of his perfection, is not affected by the seeming pleasures and pains which he regards as a mere illusion. (XXII: 39-41)

The highest jnāni makes no difference between samādhi and worldly transactions. He never finds anything apart from the Self and so there is no lapse for him. (XXII: 53)

[...] the jnāni of the highest order involuntarily and naturally abides in samādhi and any lapse is impossible for him under any circumstance. (XXII: 55)

Liberation from karma:

The jnāni of the middle order or of the highest order has no tinge of karma left in him because he is in perfection and does not perceive anything apart from the Self. How can there be anything of karma left when the wild fire of jnāna is raging, consuming all in its way? (XXII 57)

So the lowest kind of jnānis still have to deal with karma. They are the ones that go in and out of samādhi and in between are caught up in acting out karma. But out of sheer habit of entering samādhi, they will be liberated at death, if not before.

To sum up the text:

One should seek the company of the enlightened ones and hang out with them. One should study the teachings about Self-realization, such as presented in Tripura Rahasya and other texts, and ponder them. One should be devoted to the divine Mother and request Her grace. One should realize that Mother's grace is the same as Shakti, which manifests in one as kundalinī, and is the giver of bliss as well as pure intelligence (chit). One should practice self-enquiry, still the mind and practice breath control. As one begins to enter samādhi, one should ponder the different consciousness associated with samādhi and with the mind and the small self compared to the real Self. As samādhi becomes habitual, one should realize that it is still the lowest kind of enlightenment. To reach the middle state of enlightenment, the jnāni should surrender more to Mother's grace and practice entering samādhi at will and also practice upholding samādhi during activity. To move from the middle enlightenment to the highest enlightenment, one should merge with Mother's grace and not only constantly abide in the Self, but also recognize the Self in and as everything.

Shiva Sūtras

Introduction

The Shiva Sūtras date to the early ninth century AD. It is a central Kashmir Shaivism text. It was composed by Vasugupta, though said to be miraculously discovered on a rock. The text consists of three sections, known as upāyas.

Upāya is a means, a path. There are many paths, but only three manners in which these paths can be realized. The first is a spontaneous outpouring of the Self; the second is automatically by the Divine grace of the awakened Shakti within; the third is by one's own effort. These three are called shāmbhavopāya, shāktopāya and ānavopāya in the Shiva Sūtras of Kashmir Shaivism.

Shāmbhavopāya: This is the highest initiation. Here spirituality is a natural state of fulfillment.

Shāktopāya: Here spiritual practices are performed automatically by the inner workings of the awakened Shakti. Initiation into this is done by shaktipāt. It is a higher initiation than ānavopāya, but is still not the highest. In our time this is a rare thing, but there are a few shaktipāt masters around who can initiate into this path. Once on this path, one experiences the inner workings of Shakti as different from oneself, as it manifests as inner or outer kriyās. However, with time one will begin to realize one's oneness with Shakti and thus shāktopāya will transform itself into shāmbhavopāya.

Ānavaopāya: Here spiritual practices are instigated by oneself and are driven by one's own effort. This is the lowest level of initiation into spirituality. In our time, this is the most common form of spirituality.

The text and commentaries:

Chapter 1: Shāmbhavopāya: The way of Shiva

1. The Self is consciousness.

Here "consciousness" refers to pure being, not the content of the mind. In shāmbhavopāya the Self is realized as pure being, pure consciousness in and of itself; in ānavaopāya the mind is (wrongly) considered to be the self. The next sūtra assures us that the content of consciousness (knowledge) is bondage, so what is meant in this sūtra is pure consciousness in and of itself without restrictions. Also what is meant is the assurance that the Self is not unconscious. In immature nirvikalpa samādhis one may fall into unconsciousness, but later one will be fully conscious during the deepest samādhis. This is because the Self is consciousness.

2. Knowledge is bondage.

The contents of consciousness (knowledge) are not the Self; on the contrary they constitute bondage. Sūtra 1:4 says that knowledge is structured in and of language; hence the type of knowledge referred to here is discursive knowledge. Such knowledge is bondage. Discursive knowledge cannot in and of itself liberate you. Knowledge associated with the feeling of "I" and/or ownership, as in "I know this" or "this is my conviction" etc. is rooted in māyā (see next sūtra) and has no absolute validity, neither in itself nor in respect to cognizing the Self. Such knowledge comes after the I-sense has manifested itself and it covers self-cognition of the Self. This covering is technically called *āṇavamala*, where "mala" means covering and "āṇava" means primal. The primal ignorance is I-ness or I AM.

3. The source of the world whose form is activity [is also bondage].

This means māyā and activity are bondage. The source of the world is māyā and the form of activity is karma. Māyā is the source of the world and it is dynamic, not static. In sūtra 1, we were informed that the Self is consciousness in and of itself. In sūtra 2, we were informed that the contents of regular consciousness is bondage, and here in sūtra 3, we are informed that everything else is also bondage. The next sūtra informs us that the nature of ignorance is language.

4. Language is the basis of knowledge.

Language: lit.: "Mother" (*mātrikā*). "Mother" refers to the Sanskrit alphabet. Here is defined the type of bondage that is described in sūtra 2 and which is made up of knowledge: We are here told it is based in language. The Self is covered by the type of knowledge that can be put into language. Language can never grasp the Self. How, then, is the Self realized? The next sūtra explains:

5. The Self emerges.

This emergence of the Self comes about spontaneously to one who has been blessed with shaktipāt and whom the Shakti has grabbed. It is important to understand that just because one gets shaktipāt, it is not guaranteed that the Shakti will grab one. However, since we are dealing with shāmbhavopāya, there can be no doubt that Shakti has grabbed the yogi and there can thus be no question of effort. Effort is in the domain of ānavopāya. Shaktipāt is the instigator of the emergence of the Self. What happens to one in whom the Self has emerged as a conscious reality? The next sūtra answers that:

6. By merging with the wheel of energies through one-pointed meditation, the universe of plurality disappears.

This disappearing is not the end of the world; it is the end of plurality as one merges into Self-realization or even unity consciousness. Here the wheel of energies means the source of all energies, which is Shakti. Shakti projects the world onto Her own screen and the plurality of energies emerge; once one is one with Shakti, one sees through the phenomena and realizes them to be projections of Shakti. What is the nature of a yogi who has reached such a state? The next sūtra explains:

7. [The yogi] abides in the rapturous state of turyā during wakefulness, dream and deep sleep.

Turyā: the fourth state: awareness in and as the Self. Turyā is witnessing-consciousness; one constantly has a sense of the Self during all the different states of consciousness. Here turyā is used synonymously with turyātīta and simply refers to oneness with the Self. This oneness with the Self does not go away even during dream and dreamless sleep. This is Self-realization, it is not unity consciousness. If turyā, abiding in the Self, is the mark of a Self-realized person, what then constitutes wakefulness, dream and deep sleep?

8. The state of wakefulness is knowledge.

We were told knowledge is bondage and that bondage is structured in language; now we are told knowledge is the state of wakefulness. Wakefulness is characterized by discursive knowledge. Only in turyā has one transcended knowledge and rests in pure being.

9. Dreaming is vikalpas.

Vikalpas: all ideations, fluctuations and fancies of consciousness. This is also ignorance. Dreams are made up of such illusory stuff.

10. Deep sleep and māyā are characterized by lack of discernment.

"Discernment": *viveka*. Viveka means discernment in general, but also spiritual discernment between what is the Self and what is not. Though all content of the mind is absent in deep sleep, deep sleep is not a state of liberation because the primal I-ness is still intact; this primal ignorance is known as *āṇavamala*.

11. The enjoyer of the three states is master.

This enjoyment is only possible when in turyā: abiding in the Self. The Self is the master of the three states. Having explained the various states of consciousness in relation to the Self, ignorance and liberation, the text now takes a different turn and focuses on the practical aspects of how to realize the self, or of what is known as *yoga*.

12. The stations and stages of yoga are wonderful.

Yoga: "union"; means both the process of acquiring union with the Self as well as that union. First we are assured that yoga is not hard; on the contrary the various steps and stages of yoga are filled with wonder. Yogic realizations are wonderful. Remember this is shāmbhavopāya: the spontaneous and perfect yoga of supreme shaktipāt. Other yoga forms can be arduous. What is this supreme yoga like for the yogi? The next few sūtras explain:

13. [The yogi's] will is the Shakti of Shiva, which is called virgin and playful.

Virgin: "Umā", which is a name of Shakti. Here meaning untouched by the veiling power of māyā.

Playful: "Kumāri"; another name of Shakti. Here meaning the yogi's will is playful and pleasant, not arduous and tough.

Shiva: The absolute Self, one with Shakti.

The siddha yogi is suffused with Shakti. His will has merged into Shakti. It is pure delight and free of māyā. Such a yogi is liberated.

14. [To such a yogi] everything, outer or inner, is his body.

This is because such a yogi is one with Shakti and everything is Shakti. This is unity consciousness.

15. When in the heart, everything is seen as a form of consciousness.

"The heart": this is a common metaphor for the Self.

Not only is everything Shakti for such a yogi, but also Shiva (pure being, supreme consciousness). How did the yogi come to such an exalted state? The next sūtra explains:

16. Or else by constant awareness of pure being he becomes free of the binding power of limited existence.

Or else: if not already in unity consciousness.

Pure being: lit.: "pure principle (tattva)". This commonly refers to Shiva, or pure being.

Since this is shāmbhavopāya, this verse does not extol effort, but rather a spontaneous emergence of pure being in the yogi, which is the result of shaktipāt. In shaktipāt sādhana one basically meditates by observing Shakti and surrendering to the Shakti within, and this reveals Shiva.

17. Any deliberation [of such a yogi] is pure knowledge of the Self.

Deliberation: "vitarka". This means any kind of ideation or deliberation.

For such an advanced yogi, even thoughts are seen as Shakti and as the Self.

18. [Such a yogi's] joyful samādhi is blissful light.

Samādhi: Oneness with the Self.

Such samādhis are experienced just so: as bliss and light.

This verse can also be translated: "[Such a yogi's] joyful samādhi is the bliss of the universe" meaning: not only does the yogi enjoy the bliss of his samādhi, but the entire universe benefits from it: his joy is infectious.

19. Oneness with Shakti creates a body [of Shakti].

This sūtra does not mean the yogi has the supernormal power to create another body at will. It means the yogi embodies the Shakti to such a degree that he acquires a body of Shakti. It also means such a yogi can give shaktipāt initiation and create a body of Shakti in the disciple. "Body" is not to be understood too literally, but rather as an intense field of Shakti that envelops the yogi and envelops the disciple when shaktipāt is given.

139

20. [By] joining elements and separating elements: unification of the world.

"The world": *vishva* means the complete spiritual world of the yogi. The yogi's world is unified by keen discernment of the elements that constitute it. This is the process of reaching unity consciousness.

21. [By such a yogi's] perfect and pure knowledge he becomes master of the collective whole of shaktis.

Collective whole of shaktis: lit.: "universal wheel". Here is understood the many differentiated shaktis, and that the yogi becomes master of them when he is one with the supreme Shakti of Shiva in unity consciousness.

22. By merging awareness into the great ocean [of the Self, the yogi is one with] the source of all mantras.

In unity consciousness there is no need for further meditation since the yogi is one with the source of all mantras.

END OF CHAPTER 1: SHĀMBHAVOPĀYA.

If one is not an enlightened yogi in unity consciousness, what is the next best thing to do? The next chapter explains the practical aspects of shaktipāt sādhana. This concerns those who have been blessed with a weaker degree of shaktipāt than the fortunate yogis who fit in the category of shāmbhavopāya.

Chapter 2: Shāktopāya: The way of Shakti

1. The mind is mantra.

We are now exploring the practicalities of more common shaktipāt sādhana, and here one finds that the mind becomes infused with Shakti; thus the mind itself becomes mantra rather than a specific collection of letters repeated in the mind. Observing the mind as Shakti is more powerful than repeating some mantra. The last sūtra of shāmbhavopāya explained that the yogi, in unity consciousness has merged with the source of all mantras. We are now informed what the field of mantras is: the mind. During meditation, the mind becomes one with the mantra. There are numerous mantras; a short one is "om" (pronounced ohhmm). Others are "om namah Shivaya", "ham-sa" or "Shakti om", just to name a few. But one should remember that it is the mind itself that is mantra, meaning one should not simply meditate on the conglomerate of letters, but on *citta*, mind-stuff, the mind. Ultimately one has to transcend the mantra and thus the mind. In sūtra 3 we are told that "the secret of mantra is the embodiment of Self-realization."

2. Unceasing effort brings about success.

In shāktopāya a yogi is defined as one who makes an effort. In shāmbhavopāya everything is effortless. Even though we are dealing with shaktipāt sādhana, which is generally understood to be automatic, some effort is required at this level of grace. One should sit in meditation, for example.

3. The secret of mantra is the embodiment of Self-realization.

One should understand that the secret of any mantra is not its letters, but to reach the state where one embodies Self-realization. One should consider the mantra the embodiment of Shiva-Shakti; the letters should be considered to be forms of Shakti. The secret of a mantra is not to repeat the mantra in a special way or mood; it is supreme Self-realization, Shiva-Shakti. In shāktopāya the inner Shakti is the main thing and what one should surrender to. In sūtra II:1 we were told the mind is mantra. Does this mean that the mind is the embodiment of Self-realization? No, it does not. It means the external form of the mantra is mind, while the "secret of mantra is the embodiment of Self-realization". What happens if one does not understand this secret of mantra? The next sūtra explains:

4. [The yogi whose] mind is satisfied with illusion falls to the realm of common dreamlike knowledge.

In shāmbhavopāya a fall is not possible. In shāktopāya such a fall is unfortunately possible if one relapses to the level of ānavopāya. What happens to the one who does not fall? Next sūtra explains:

5. On the spontaneous emergence of supreme knowledge [of the Self], moving in the vast expanse of consciousness, the state of Shiva [is established].

In sūtra I:5 we were told that emergence of transcendental awareness is the Self. Now we are told this emergence is a natural and spontaneous thing; this emergence comes about by the awakened Shakti through shaktipāt. Surrender to Shakti is the means to Shiva in shāktopāya. How does one get the Shakti going to such a degree that one can surrender to it? Are there any means? The next sūtra answers:

6. The guru is the means.

This is because the guru, the enlightened master who brings one from darkness to light, grants the disciple shaktipāt. Shakti then leads the disciple along shāktopāya to shāmbhavopāya. In ānavopāya the means are various practices.

7. Understanding of the wheel of letters [is given by the guru].

Wheel of letters: the Sanskrit alphabet. Mantras are made up of letters and the meanings of them are given by the guru. The mother of the sounds of the alphabet is kundalinī; so this verse indirectly states that the guru gives knowledge of kundalinī through mantra. Some shaktipāt gurus give shaktipāt through a mantra, others through touch, sight or an inanimate object.

8. The body is the offering.

When initiated into shaktipāt, the energy of kundalinī "burns" (purifies) the body, thus making it an offering to the Self.

9. Knowledge is the food.

In I:2 we were told that knowledge is bondage. Now we are told that it is the food of the offering. This is because one in shāmbhavopāya has transcended limited knowledge and understands it to be bondage. In shāktopāya one is in the process of transcending limited knowledge and in this process limited knowledge becomes consumed in the fire of Shakti.

10. On losing his Self-understanding [the yogi] relapses into a dreamlike state.

Just because one is on the path of shāktopāya, one cannot be sure not to fall. If such a fall happens one relapses to ānavopāya; the subject of the next chapter.

END OF CHAPTER 2: SHĀKTOPĀYA.

Chapter 3: Ānavopāya: The way of the individual

1. The self is the mind.

The mind here means I-ness, understanding and thinking. This is the state of ignorance one confronts in ānavopāya. One considers oneself to be the mind and has no inkling of the Self.

2. Knowledge is bondage.

The situation described in sūtra 1 is here elaborated. Mind-born knowledge is not a source of liberation; it is a source of bondage and has to be transcended. In I:2 we were also told that knowledge is bondage, but there it meant that the yogi had transcended it, here it means that the yogi is identified with it.

3. Māyā is non-distinction of the tattvas such as kalā.

Māyā is the grand illusion of taking the constitutive elements to be the Self.

Tattvas are the 31 constitutive principles. Some say there are 36. The number is not so important.

Kalā is one such tattva: it is limited doership.

146

4. [Distinction comes about by] dissolution of kalā [etc.] in the body.

Here "body" means all the separate principles that make up the ignorant individual from basic I-ness to the physical body. One imagines they all dissolve and leaves absolutely nothing left. The body becomes a void in a void. The next sūtra gives a different method:

5. Dissolution [of the prāna] from the nādis [into sushumna], control over the elements, withdrawal from the elements and separation from the elements.

"Dissolution from the nādis" can only mean of prāna, which flows in the nādis, and dissolution can only mean the dissolution of prāna that happens when prāna enters the spine. This is a description of awakening kundalinī and bringing it into the spine and up to the brain. Once that is accomplished in its full extent, one will soon move from ānavopāya to shāktopāya and then to shāmbhavopāya. Following is one such method we call kundalinī prānāyāma:

Practice:

Here you follow and control your breath. You breathe in, hold your breath and breathe out. That is one round, then you breathe in again, etc. In-breath, holding and out-breath should be of equal duration; typically a count of three is fine and allows one to do this prāṇāyāma for a long time. Instead of counting one could mentally recite the mantra "Om Aim Hrim Klim" or any other mantra. Important: On the in-breath sense you are awakening kundalinī and bringing it up the spine to the brain, sense energy flowing up the spine. While holding the breath, sense energy radiating from the brain. On the out-breath continue to sense energy radiating from the brain. Do this uninterrupted for 45 minutes twice daily and results will soon come. It is important to do it uninterrupted, so time the speed you count carefully.

6. Due to a veil of ignorance siddhis [arise].

Siddhis are perfect abilities or rather, supernormal powers. One should not be content with siddhis, because one is still bound by the great illusion, māyā, of taking non-Self for Self. The only interesting siddhi is the power to give shaktipāt, because that transcends māyā. The ability to give shaktipāt arises by itself as one progresses.

7. After conquering infinite delusion, mastery of natural wisdom arises.

Mastery of natural wisdom (Self-realization) does not arise due to siddhis, but only due to conquering māyā (infinite delusion) and its impressions (samskaras). This conquering takes place in meditation.

8. [Then] wakefulness is another form of one's effulgent light.

One's effulgent light: The purity of natural wisdom, i.e. Self-realization. This is the state of Self-realization in wakefulness, not just in meditation. It is thus true Self-realization and is the goal of ānavopāya. What is it like to be Self-realized? The following sūtras elaborate:

9. The Self is an actor.

Actor could also be translated "dancer". In both cases the meaning is the same: The world, and life, is a play of consciousness. Though the Self appears as you it is not you, it is You. Meaning the Self adopts the act of the small, individual personality, but it is really not that personality; it is the absolute, unmanifest Self. This is how it appears in basic Self-realization. Ānavopāya can only lead to basic Self-realization. Shāktopāya can lead to god-consciousness. Shāmbhavopāya can lead to unity consciousness. In god-consciousness one sees everything manifest as Shakti. In unity consciousness one sees everything as the Self.

10. The innermost Self is the stage.

Not only is the Self the actor, but the act is performed on the stage of the Self. Sūtras 9 and 10 remind us of sūtra 2 of Pratyabhijñāhridayam: "By Her own will She unfolds the universe upon Her own screen".

11. The senses are the spectators.

The yogi's senses are not a source of bondage but of enjoyment as they perceive Shakti's act. Also "spectator" implies that there is no involvement in the drama unfolding on the scene; one is a witness, a spectator, not a participant.

12. The light of the Self is realized through supreme understanding.

Though the senses are the spectators of the act of the Self, they cannot realize the Self. Only supreme understanding can realize the Self. Some misguided commentators claim the Self is realized by the power of the intellect; however the intellect can by its very nature not grasp the Self.

13. [Thus] freedom is achieved.

Once the Self has been realized freedom is achieved.

14. As in the body, so elsewhere.

Just as the yogi can achieve freedom within the limits of his own body, so he can find freedom in every part of his individual make-up: the emotions, the mind, etc. In god-consciousness and unity consciousness he can even find it in creation; however, it is unlikely that is what is meant here, since we are in ānavopāya. This freedom within the body is possible because the Self is an actor on its own stage and the senses are the spectators of that act. How can this Self-realization be achieved? The next sūtra explains:

15. The focus of attention should be on the seed.

The seed: The supreme Shakti. In the light of the preceding sūtras the seed can be either the seed of the world, which is Shakti, or it can be the seed of understanding, which is also Shakti. One should focus one's attention on the supreme Shakti in order to realize the Self "in the body as elsewhere".

16. Easily established in right posture [the yogi] plunges into the lake [of the Self].

Right posture: Right spiritual posture is oneness with Shakti. Concerning a physical posture for meditation, we are here told that it is something easy: pick any comfortable position. Sitting cross-legged is common for meditation but by no means a must.

17. Consciousness takes form after what one has brought about [through meditation].

After plunging into the Self, one's conscious understanding of Self and self will change according to what one can bring back into everyday wakeful awareness. Even one's understanding of what consciousness is will change drastically. In the beginning, while ignorant, consciousness is seen as one's private sphere of personal identity, of ego. Later, in Self-realization, consciousness is seen as a manifestation of pure being. The ultimate change is of

152

course to become fully established in the Self throughout all states of consciousness. What happens when one is established in the Self? The next sūtra informs us:

18. Once established in the Self, rebirths cease.

What is it that binds one in rebirth? The next sūtra explains:

19. The mothers of the bondage of the soul reside in "ka" and the other consonants of the alphabet.

This strange sūtra deals with Kashmir Shaivism metaphysics and language theory. It is best understood metaphorically for the power language holds over awareness. In I:4 we were told that language is the basis of the type of knowledge that holds one in ignorance. Is there a state that transcends the lure of language? Yes, the "fourth state": turyā. The next sūtra explains:

20. The fourth state [of consciousness] should be poured into the other three like oil.

The fourth state: "turyā". The other three are wakefulness, dream and deep sleep. Turyā is oneness with the Self. In I:7 we were told

153

that the fully enlightened yogi "abides in the rapturous state of turyā during wakefulness, dream and deep sleep." Here we are told that the not yet enlightened yogi should practice upholding turyā during the other three states. The way of upholding turyā should be like pouring oil; meaning in a calm, steady and continuous manner without the slightest interruption or wavering. This is easier said than done. How does one do it? The next sūtra explains:

21. One should plunge into turyā without any thought construct.

Thoughts may be there, but they cannot enter or grasp turyā, so they are to be left behind. It is the mind's nature to think, so just leave the thoughts alone; don't try to stop the mind. If you succeed in stopping the mind, you will not on that account enter turyā, you will merely have a quiet mind. One should simply let go of the thoughts and dive into pure being. Does the text give any other hints? The next sūtra does:

22. When the prāna slowly spreads out, awareness of everything's oneness arises.

Prāna: the vital force of the body that follows breath. It is a condensed form of Shakti and can be used as a gateway to plunge into turyā.

Everything's oneness: When one with Shakti, one will experience Shakti in and as everything so oneness will be a reality.

The following practices are part of kundalinī kriyā meditation:

Practice I:
Sense the entire body. Follow your breathing as it comes and goes by itself. On the in-breath sense your energy field (prāna) spreads out around the body and you become larger and the energy becomes more intense. On the out-breath simply let go. With some practice this simple meditation will take one to turyā and the bliss of the Self.

Practice II:
Sense the spine and the center of the brain. Sense energy flows into this all over and from all directions and heats it. Simultaneously, sense energy radiates from it in all directions. This is a very powerful practice; do not underestimate it.

23. In the intervening stage inferior states arise.

The intervening stage: what comes after one has left turyā and before one enters it again. When out of turyā, one relapses into inferior states of consciousness. Is everything then to be lost again? No, every bit of practice helps. The next two sūtras explain:

24. When lost, Self-awareness rises again when objects are united with the Self.

Self-awareness (turyā) will be lost again and again. However, one should not despair, for it will come again repeatedly if one perseveres. The means to return to samādhi, when one loses it during meditation, is to focus on the objects of awareness that has pulled one out and see them as Shakti and then plunge back into the Self; this is to unite objects with the Self. What happens when one repeatedly enters samādhi? The next sūtra explains:

25. [One then] becomes like Shiva.

The means to realize one's oneness with Shiva/Shakti is to repeatedly enter samādhi. The following sūtras explain what life is like for such a Self-realized being:

26. Remaining in the body one performs pious acts.

27. [Such a one's] speech is like mantra-recitation.

28. [Such a one's] charity is [disseminating] knowledge of the Self.

29. [Such a one, who is] established [in the Self], surely is an agent of Self-realization.

30. [Such a one experiences] the universe as a manifestation of His Shakti.

"His Shakti" means Shiva-Shakti, not the individual yogi's personal energy.

31. Persistence and absorption.

Not only is the universe experienced as Shiva-Shakti, but so is the persistence and absorption of impressions. Such persistence and absorption is common to all, but only the accomplished yogi can follow them from and back to Shiva-Shakti. Why? The next sūtra explains:

32. Despite this [persistence and absorption] there is no break in the Self-realization.

The accomplished yogi is a witness to the fluctuations in his consciousness due to his absorption in the Self.

33. [Such a one] considers pleasure and pain as external [to the Self].

The Self is a witness to pleasure and pain and thus the accomplished yogi considers them as outside of his being. This does not mean such a yogi does not subjectively experience pleasure and pain from time to time, but it means his Self-understanding as one with pure Being is prior to such fluctuations.

34. Free from pleasure and pain [since such a one is] established in the Self alone.

Again, it should be clear that such a yogi subjectively can experience pleasure and pain like anybody else, but his Self, his pure being, is unaffected by them since he as such is a witness to them. How does this contrast with one who is not Self-realized? The next sūtra answers that:

158

35. But [one who is] completely deluded [is] caught up in karma.

"Caught up in karma": identified with performing good and bad deeds and experiencing such. Also suffering the consequences of past actions as a certain fate one has to live through.

36. On the removal of difference another reality is created.

Such a deluded person has to transcend his differentiating perception and again merge awareness into oneness with Shiva-Shakti. Once one with the Self and having transcended pleasure and pain, the yogi will have left the deluded reality behind and entered a new reality. So does this sūtra mean the yogi has a unique power to create things? The next sūtra answers:

37. The power to create is experienced by everyone.

This sūtra makes it clear that the accomplished yogi does not have any unusual power to manifest things and that such an interpretation of the previous sūtra is wrong.

38. The three states [of consciousness] should be enlivened by the pre-eminent state [of turyā].

Three states of consciousness: Wakefulness, dream and deep sleep.

Turyā: Oneness with the Self.

As mentioned in III:20 one should pour turyā into the other three states of consciousness like oil (in a steady and stable manner). This repetitive verse drives the point, touched in sūtra III:36 and others, home: that repeated diving into turyā is the way out of delusion and into Self-realization.

39. Just as the [three] states of consciousness, [so should] the body, the sense-organs and the external world [be enlivened by turyā].

Turyā can also be used to transform the body, the sense-organs and the external world. One should not, when attempting such, begin to be motivated by want. The next sūtra explains why not. Please see the practices described under III:22.

40. Due to feeling want [the deluded one is] extroverted and carried from birth to birth.

Extroverted: Pulled out of the state of turyā, out of the Self.

41. For the one who is Self-realized such [delusion] has ended and the state of being limited has ended.

I have inserted "delusion", however, one could also insert that reincarnation has ended. This sūtra does not mean the limited personality vanishes. It is still there for the rest of the present incarnation. It means one is thoroughly out of the sphere of personhood, never to be caught up in it again.

42. Then, for him who uses the body comprised of the gross elements as a mere covering, there is a perfect state of liberation, like Shiva.

You are not your body. The body is merely a container you have incarnated into. In fact you have never incarnated at all, you are pure being that has never been tainted by incarnations. Yet, while alive, the body for a Self-realized yogi is merely a covering, a shell.

43. He is naturally linked with the prāna.

161

Prāna: In- and out-breath, and vital currents in the body.

The next sūtra explains what is meant:

44. With prāna-shakti established in the sushumnā rather than the left and right channels, [such a yogi abides in] the centre of inner consciousness.

Left and right channels: On either side of the spine there is a channel, *idā* to the left and *pingalā* to the right.

Please see the practices described under III:5 and III:22.

45. Again and again [such a yogi] has the awareness of the Divine both within and without.

END OF CHAPTER 3: ĀNAVOPĀYA.

THUS CONCLUDES THE SHIVA-SUTRAS

Prior to Silence

1. The mind is noise, realization is silent

When reading about silence, understand you are indulging in noise. Writings about silence can only be so many noisy pointers; like writings about the Self. The Self is prior to silence: Silence may be taken to mean absence of noise; in the Self there is no absence and nothing to be absent from; hence we are prior to silence.

Silence is initially understood to be absence of noise; ultimately to be just above the essence of our Being. For so many the essence of Being is sadly assumed to be noise of some sort, or pleasant turbulence. People identify with noise: They assume: If there is noise, there is ego and cognition, *cogito ergo sum* (I think therefore I am) as Descartes wrote; the truth is *cogito ergo occultum* (I think therefore I am hidden from myself). In fear of losing their ego, people worship noise or turbulence. Examples of worshiped noise are fanatical bhakti or fanatical jnāna; in fact it could be any practice or attitude that gives you a good kick of feeling good about yourself or your spiritual endeavors or sādhana.

The nature of the mind is to scrutinize and doubt, not to realize and be. Doubt is noise; so is faith, devotion and knowledge. Realization is silent; the mind is noise. Anything that can be verbalized is more or less junk with respect to getting Self-realized.

When people long for silence, they usually long for a quiet mind. However, they will be disappointed: Quietness of the mind is only temporary; such is the nature of the mind.

Silencing the mind is in itself useless with regard to becoming Self-realized. However, it may help setting the stage necessary for revelation to occur.

Insights are not silent; revelations originate in silence. People have this mixed up. Ecstasy is extremely turbulent. Ecstasy comes before immergence into pure Being and thus before silence. However, this ecstasy charms you to believe it is the Self.

There are three silences: One prior to ecstasy, one posterior to ecstasy and one transcending ecstasy and the two afore mentioned silences.

There are no beliefs within radical silence and no believer; nothing to yearn for and nothing to flee from. It is unmanifest; this unmanifest is You.

2. Silent mind is not the Self

No-mind enhances spiritual pride in a subtle manner; so does bhakti, so does jnāna, and so forth. Let go of them all.

164

Silent mind is not in itself oneness with the Self, it is merely a state of no-thought or no-mind. There can be oneness with the Self and yet thoughts. The important thing is to disidentify with thoughts and the mind, whether the mind is silent or not. The most important thing is to transcend identifications and realize you already are the Self.

You are not even silence. You are prior to silence.

3. Disidentification is challenging

Initially, when radical silence enters one's conscious awareness, disidentification may be challenging.

When disidentification challenges you, functioning properly may become difficult. Who is operating? No one! Thus motivation is no longer present.

When motivation is lost, a phase of spiritual apathy sets in. This occurs in the dark night of the mind.

The dark night of the mind concerns deconstruction of beliefs; the dark night of the soul concerns deconstruction of the believer.

4. Practice is noise

Meditation-practices are all noise to some extent. Understand that in order to reach the silence of the Self, you have to let go of your practice, whatever it may be. There is no exception to this: All practices must go, even bhakti.

In meditation, every spiritual state that is not samādhi is either practice or distraction.

All spiritual practices should aim at setting the stage for revelation to occur; if they do not, they are merely noise or satisfying rituals, which amounts to the same.

In themselves all spiritual practices are noise; they should aim at transcending themselves, otherwise they are merely mood-making or preparing the ground.

No mood is conducive to Self-realization. All are just dreams. Moods and dreams may quiet the mind and heart, or put the mind and heart in a nice state, but they will not lead to transcendental immergence in the Self.

However some moods are more conducive to transcending noise than others; hence various yogas, disciplines and attitudes are preferred. Bhakti is a good mood, but it can also be a prison. Radical bhakti, parabhakti, is generated by Shakti as a deep devotion to Shiva (the Self).

166

Silence is not the goal. You need to go prior to silence in order to find the Self.

In the Self there is no turbulence, no noise, no fluctuation of any sort; hence no absence of noise; hence no silence. Yet it is the source of all turbulence and joy.

Don't worry about what is the right way to meditate or pray, just remember you have to transcend each and every way possible. Prayer is a beneficial kind of noise in as far as it transcends itself; if not it is merely begging. Spiritual begging is detrimental to transcendence.

Surrender!

5. Silence is not void; void is not silence

With experience one realizes silence is not void; one realizes it is supreme bliss; silent bliss.

When not Self-realized and silent, life's inherent meaninglessness will inevitably become obvious. This will frustrate the mind and heart. Do not give up your sādhana at this stage. Later the meaninglessness will go away and be replaced with loving no-meaning. Differentiate between no-meaning and meaningless.

Immature silence debilitates the mind and memory. It is not to be cultivated; but it is a common phase prior to Self-realization.

When in this phase, do not panic, but let go and surrender to Shakti.

6. You can be one with the Self, yet have a noisy mind

The nature of the Self is prior to silence and this prior-to-silence is blissful. Understand that though the Self may be silent, and though union with the Self may be silent, the mind may still make its usual noise. So there are two levels: One of silence and one of noise; the important thing is to disidentify with noise and fall into silence. Once in silence, you have to go prior to silence into void. Or jump directly from noise to void if you can.

In meditation, when one first enters samādhi, the mind may go berserk and create an awful lot of noise. The heart will beat wildly, thoughts come and go rapidly, the eyelids will flicker, and so forth. But behind this, depending on the level of samādhi, one rests in void. This void may not be too apparent as prior to silence, but it is.

Mind may become ecstatic when first suffused with Shakti, but that is just a phase. Truth is silent. Mind cannot grasp silent truth. The Self is prior to truth and thus prior to silence.

Though pure awareness may be one with the love and bliss of the Self, the mind may become frustrated; it is a common misconception that this should not be so.

168

7. Shakti is prior to silence

Shakti is the potential dynamism of the unmanifest, hence it is prior to silence understood as prior to absence of noise. Shakti is the creative potential.

Shakti is not a burst of energy. Kinetic energy is noise and turbulence. Shakti is the potential dynamism of the Self in a yet unmanifest state. When Shakti bursts forth and begins to manifest in and as the individual, it is kundalinī.

To fully realize Shakti is to realize the Self.

Initially silence is devoid of bliss. Later bliss becomes realized as noise, in ecstasy. Ultimately bliss and silence are one. Shakti is bliss prior to silence; this is the Self.

Objectless love and radical silence are one with pure being.

Mother's Grace

The Self realizes itself; it is not that you somehow grow into Self-realization. Please understand this sentence; meditate on it. Ignorance is the false belief that you are the body and/or the mind. Strictly speaking you do not get rid of ignorance, you step into clear understanding. It is not that clear understanding grows; it is already perfect within you as the Self. A clear mind can be developed, but being a clear mind it is just as ignorant as being an unclear mind. It may, however, be easier to step into clear understanding with a clear mind than with a cloudy mind, but not necessarily so. An unclear mind may be so massive that it is plain obvious what pure being is compared with it. On the other hand a clear mind may easily believe itself to be almost enlightened, which it can never be.

Mother, or Divine Mother, is the grace of the Self that seemingly separates itself from the Self as a force acting for your liberation. It is, however, never separate from the Self as liberation is the Self that realizes itself. Such is grace that the bliss of the Self assumes a form understandable from the ignorant perspective in order to establish Self-realization. Mother resides within you as kundalinī. Surrender to Mother as kundalinī; surrender to Mother as the bliss of the Self; there is no difference. Even if you know nothing of kundalinī, if you are overwhelmed by major bliss in meditation, it is kundalinī answering your prayer by infusing your brain with Shakti. This is the case even with minor bliss, though this may be an infusion with prāna (vital force) rather than Shakti. Prāna is kundalinī-shakti within the relative, assuming the role as vital force, while Shakti is the dynamic aspect of pure being. Prāna is a manifestation of kundalinī.

Love cannot hide from this. If a person has realized the Self, but is not in great love, then the Self-realization is internal only, in the form of void, and thus of the lowest kind. It is better than nothing, but naught but the beginning of the unfoldment of the Self. The medium kind of Self-realization has also realized the Self internally, but in addition sees Mother in everything and lives in love. The highest kind of Self-realization no longer distinguishes between Mother and Self; this is unity consciousness and is very difficult to reach. In this state everything is seen as the Self and one is One with Mother, not as a simple unity of two, but as in no distinction what so ever.

Death no longer frightens a Self-realized person, as he knows his immortality.

Discussions of matters as outlined above are important, but if they are not followed by proper effort, they are fruitless. Logic can be an aid as well as a hindrance. Proper effort is more important than logic. Logic is of three kinds: It can point beyond itself by falling into the Self; it can confirm itself by falling into the mind; it can play with itself by falling back into similar lines of thought. In the completely ignorant mind, the third, latter, form of logic is praised as the highest. The medium kind of logic is found in immature seekers, who have not yet experienced the Self. The first kind of logic is found in seekers who know the Self well or who have realized the Self and wish to teach. Logic that points beyond itself is of no use, however, if it does not lead to proper effort.

Proper effort means proper practice. Proper practice is always simple as it should be an invitation to the Self to realize itself, and not be an exercise of the mind or body. Proper practice is always to surrender to Mother. Mother is the Self of all and She can be reached effortlessly or with effort. Effortless practice is to merge with bliss that wells up within. Effortful practice is to raise kundalinī for the sake of getting bliss to well up within. Pure grace is when an enlightened master awakens one's kundalinī so it will grant one Self-realization; this is known as shaktipāt. There is no initiation higher than shaktipāt.

Faith is important. Without any realization, faith in teachings along the line of the above is all-important. Proper practice in such a case relies on faith. It takes faith to let go of one's identity and dive into the Self. Courage is required. Those without courage to test the above teachings through proper effort are difficult to awake. They can only be awakened through Mother's grace which comes in the form of shaktipāt. Not all can receive shaktipāt.

Shaktipāt is one with Mother's grace; not like two fused together, but as in one and the same. Anyone who gives shaktipāt is an instrument of Mother's grace. Anyone who receives shaktipāt is offered Mother's grace. However, not everyone who receives shaktipāt receives Mother's grace; grace may, so to speak, not be able to penetrate the layers of identification on the part of the recipient. The recipient should have deep rooted faith in shaktipāt for Mother's grace to grab hold of the recipient; or the recipient should have an intuitive understanding of all the above; or the recipient should know what proper effort is and practice it; or the recipient should simply have given up and be in a state of surrender. Surrender requires faith. Giving up without faith is hopelessness, not proper surrender.

How do you know you are temporarily united with Mother? You sense, know, feel your body and mind to be manifestations of pure bliss-Shakti. You are one with this bliss-Shakti and perceive the body and mind as external from you.

In the absence of bliss, zeal is what counts. The seeker profits according the zeal he puts into proper effort. In the presence of bliss, surrender is what counts. This means that when a seeker who does not habitually experience bliss, suddenly experiences bliss, he should immediately stop what he is doing and surrender to the bliss. Bliss in meditation is not a result of the practice, but is a result of Mother's grace, so give up the practice and surrender.

Bliss comes when kundalinī flows into the brain. Linguistically, "kundalinī" means "the coiled one" and in general kundalinī is indeed "coiled". This can be understood both literally, as coiled up in the root chakra (slightly above the perineum), as well as metaphorically, as in an awkward position incapable of rising. Kundalinī needs to be awakened in order for it to straighten out and enter the spine. When asleep, kundalinī only maintains the bodily functions, the mind and the feelings and what else comes with being human. In other words, while asleep, kundalinī maintains one's state of ignorance.

When incarnating, kundalinī interacts with the fetus and descends into the budding central nervous system while the fetus develops. First kundalinī develops the crown chakra and all that is associated with that, then the so called third eye, etc. all the way down until it reaches the lowest chakra, where it "falls asleep". This structures one's personality in conjunction with the body, and thus makes up one's structure of ignorance. When kundalinī awakens, the reverse process takes place and kundalinī begins to undo one's ignorance. Kundalinī undoes the knots in one's system and removes the layers of dirt, that keep one's awareness in ignorance, until finally kundalinī reaches the brain and gives bliss. First kundalinī gets dissolved into the central nervous system and then finally merges with pure being in the brain. This reverse process is Mother's grace. This may sound mysterious in the light of this more technical description of kundalinī as asleep and awakened, but one will realize for oneself that Mother's grace is the only way to handle the immense bliss and love that fills one's heart and soul. The fastest and safest way to awaken kundalinī is shaktipāt. Shaktipāt is Mother's grace.

Kundalinī is known by different names according to what state it is in. The pure, liberated kundalinī, one with pure being, is called para-kundalinī. When para-kundalinī manifests in the individual, it is called shakti-kundalinī, or kundalinī-shakti, or just kundalinī for short. Kundalinī-shakti manifests prāna-kundalinī and chit-kundalinī. Prāna-kundalinī (or prāna for short) makes up all the vital forces and the breath, while chit-kundalinī makes up the consciousness of the individual. When united with para-kundalinī, one's awareness has merged into the unity of pure being and Shakti, and this state is known as nirvikalpa samādhi. Any form of kundalinī is a valid way to reach para-kundalinī, or samādhi. This means that valid efforts consist of employing kundalinī-shakti in order to reach para-kundalinī, and that kundalinī-shakti can be stimulated by chit-kundalinī or prāna-kundalinī for one's spiritual advancement. Employing chit-kundalinī is known as meditation and employing prāna-kundalinī is known as prānāyāma. In all cases one must leave the form of kundalinī one begins with and move on to para-kundalinī, which is supreme bliss. In other words, no matter what one's method or practice may be, one must give it up at the right moment and surrender to bliss. This brings us back to Mother's grace. When kundalinī awakens all yogas begin to manifest spontaneously in one and one fulfills all yogas, thus the yoga of kundalinī shaktipāt is known as perfect yoga (siddha yoga) and the greatest yoga (maha yoga). The only initiation to this is shaktipāt.

Mother's grace is what takes you from method to bliss. You cannot take this step by yourself, since you let go of doing. You cannot do anything to merge with bliss. Bliss pulls you into itself and this pull is Mother's grace. All you have to do is let go and surrender to the sense of bliss and the sense of Shakti.

You do not have to win Mother's grace, it is there in abundance, waiting. You have to open yourself to it. Mother's grace would not be perfect, if it had not already placed within you the key to surrendering to her grace. This key is kundalinī. However, when kundalinī is asleep, the key is hidden, so to speak. Oh, seeker! Awaken kundalinī! Oh, Mother! Awaken kundalinī in everyone!

Pray, seeker, for your kundalinī to awaken. Pray to Mother to grant you that boon; and once She grants it, everything will progress by itself from then on. Internally it will progress smoothly, but from the point of view of the mind and the body, it may or may not be a smooth ride. Kriyās may manifest; they usually do. Kriyās can be spontaneous movements of the arms or other parts of the body. Or it may be spontaneous mutterings of sounds or even screaming. Or it may be a gentle shivering of the spine as Shakti moves up to your brain. Kriyās are innumerable. They are signs of internal purification, but don't think that if there are no apparent kriyās, there is no purification. Trust Shakti, surrender to Shakti and surrender to bliss. Once kundalinī has awakened, that is all you have to do.

If you want to start with chit-kundalinī, do meditation. Remember the goal of meditation is to awaken kundalinī. Why? Because kundalinī is the grace of Mother, that will pull you into the Self. You can do meditation and control your thoughts to perfection, but that will in itself only lead to a blank mind. You have to transcend the notions of "mine" and "my". You may reach a perfectly blank mind, but as long as you think of it as "my mind", it will do no good. You may then transcend the notion of "my" and be absorbed in the void of the blank mind – some believe that is enlightenment; however, it is not, no matter how permanent and stable the void is. If kundalinī-shakti is not awakened, void will eventually go away and become noisy again. If not in this life, then in the next as karma manifests a new mind for you to grapple with.

The notion of "my" needs to be analyzed at some point by every seeker. It is obvious that what you think of as "my spouse" is really a relationship and not an ownership. But it is more tricky when it comes to your thoughts. Realize that your thoughts are not yours! Thoughts happen. Just like the beating heart that does what is has to do to take care of the body, the mind does what is has to do to take care of the body: it thinks. There is nothing wrong with thoughts, just don't claim ownership of them. Analyze everything in this way and what remains is the Self. However, this kind of analysis is very difficult to take to the end, and self-enquiry is a very cumbersome way. Mother's grace is nicer, more blissful, sweeter and faster.

You may arrest your thoughts completely and think this is the goal. You may enter void-consciousness and think that is the goal. However, something has to happen in the void to take you into the supreme. A blazing light with no circumference must temporarily fill the void. This is Mother's grace. Once you have had this inner blazing light initiation by Mother's grace, you will have a somewhat active kundalinī and be on the way to Self-realization; at least as a budding start.

When meditating, control your mind a little. Do not fight with it. First notice you are extroverted, then become introverted, then control the mind a little and do your meditation. When meditating, you may silently repeat the mantra "klimm". Do not make the repetition into the practice, because that will lead nowhere. Use every repetition of the mantra as a chance to see the source of the mantra, which is the Self. If you just sit "klimm, klimm, klimm …" nothing will happen. Every time you think the mantra, think it gently and silently and think it as if every time is the first. You may receive the blazing inner light initiation. If you don't like Klimm, you can use Om or Aing instead or any other short Tantric mantra, such as Aim or Hrim.

Similarly prāṇāyāma may lead to the blazing inner light initiation. First notice you are extroverted, then become introverted, then control the mind a little and do your prāṇāyāma.

Gently breathe in at the count of three or four. Then hold your breath for the same period. Then gently breathe out for the same period. This is one round. Do as many rounds as you wish. When breathing in, imagine Shakti flowing up the spine and into the brain. When you hold your breath and when you breathe out, imaging Shakti radiating from the brain in all directions. May this simple prānāyāma quickly awaken your kundalinī and fill you with bliss.

Practice should always be simple. Complicated practices will involve the mind too much for the mind to be easily transcended.

Pure being, or Shiva, is absolute awareness without any content, and thus formless. Shakti is one with pure being. Shakti may take any form but will never lose its status of pure being. The union of Shiva and Shakti is perfection. In the beginning it may seem that Shakti is the means and Shiva is the goal, but in truth, Shakti is itself the goal, only one has to realize the Shiva-ness of Shakti. Merging Shakti into Shiva, or realizing the Shiva-ness of Shakti develops into the same state of enlightenment, for ultimately, it is the same state of Oneness of Shiva-Shakti-Self.

Song of Liberation

Stanzas and comments by the author.

> **1. The highest internal realization is indescribable because it is free of I-ness and something-ness. You can say it is the Self, but you cannot say it is "me", because there is no longer a "me", or an "I", in that unmanifest purity of being. "Me" and "I" are of course identical, while "the Self" is your penultimate being and separate.**

There are higher realizations which can be described as external; these will be described later. The highest internal realization is freedom from I-ness and complete and utter merging of Self-awareness in the Self. One can only vaguely use the word "Self" to describe this internal state since any word used will limit the described, and pure being is at best described as unmanifest and therefore limitless. It is a curious quality of the Self that it can no longer be referenced as a "me", this is also because the Self is unmanifest. There is no "me", there is simply pure, unmanifest being. The Self is separate from the common "me". The "me" and the "I" are identical since they refer to the same personality. When Self-realized, one's awareness has transcended the "I" and the "me" and has dissolved in the Self. In this dissolving, awareness realizes that not only is the Self its source, but is its very nature and essence. There is nothing higher than the Self since it is unmanifest and one's penultimate pure being. Thus the highest internal realization is of the Self. Yet all this is very well; the penultimate pure being is unmanifest and therefore indescribable.

2. The penultimate Self cannot be said to be yours; you cannot say "my pure being". This is because pure being transcends "you"; it is simply "pure being" and ownership implies duality. It is more right to say that the "you" belongs to the Self, just as "I" and "I AM" do. When you become Self-realized this feature is very prominent: speaking as pure being, the "me" is an exterior object that belongs to you. You can say "my me" and be expressing a concrete experience, not just an absurd play of words. The "me" is not you, but you live in the world through it. It belongs to you in the loosest sense of the word, though nothing really can belong to pure Being since it has no ownership.

Similarly one cannot claim ownership of the Self. This is because it is one's very Self and thus the ultimate owner. If one owned the Self there would be duality, which there is not. What is commonly termed "me" and "I", is something that really does not own, though it thinks it is the owner. Rather it is owned by the Self, though it does commonly not recognize this. But the Self does really not own anything since it is unmanifest. But the contrast between pre- and post-realization is stark, and where one before thought of pure being as one's own, one as Self-realized gets a clear sense that the personality, the "I" and "me", belong to one as relative phenomena. In reality they do not belong to one, since there is no ownership in the Self. Here we are introduced to I AM as something in the same category of relative identity as "me" and "I". There is a widespread tendency to identify I AM as the Self; however, it is not. This verse makes it clear that I AM is more related to the relative "I" than to the penultimate Self.

3. Sometimes the highest state is said to be I AM, but it is not so. As long as there's an I that IS, there is identification with it and there is I-ness, so it is not the highest internal realization of the Self.

This verse makes it clear that I AM is as far from the Self as the common personality known as the "I" is. In fact I-ness is such an intrinsic part of I AM, that I AM is inseparable from the basic identification that characterizes common ignorance of the Self. It is therefore plainly stated that I AM is not the highest internal realization spoken of in the previous verse. I-ness and

182

identification are inseparable and they are also inseparable from an "I" that is. One cannot have one without the other two.

4. Out of pure being arises "I-ness". Out of "I-ness" arises "I AM". Out of "I AM" arises the "me". You can identify with any level that arises out of something else, but identification with pure being is not possible because it is prior to I-ness. Identification needs I-ness, so the I-ness can be said to also be the identification-principle, and the primal identification is I AM where I-ness becomes self-referential.

I-ness can be said to be prior to I AM, since I-ness is needed for the self-aware notion of the "I" to arise. Thus I AM is not even the finest relative realization or principle to be transcended. Self-realization is not a matter of changing identity or identification from something to something more essentially you. Self-realization has nothing to do with identities and identifications at all. Pure being is a witness to all identities and identifications; however, it is never part of them. Where does identification come from? It arises out of a sense of I-ness that is the first manifestation out of pure being. When I-ness arises it immediately becomes self-referential and at once identification and I AM arise simultaneously. Thus I AM and primal ego are inseparate, since ego rests in I-ness and identification.

5. There is nothing enlightened about I AM at all. It is not a small point about to burst and suddenly throw you into pure being. It is more like a massive fog permeating every part of your mind and spirit with ego. I AM is not the entry-point to enlightenment, it is the prime source of ignorance.

It is a gross mistake that I AM should be the essential Self. In fact, I AM is the source and basis of ignorance about the Self. It is not even that I AM is a subtle boundary to the Self; rather I AM is a principle that permeates each and every aspect of ego. As you transcend the mind and approach the Self, it is not that you reach more and more subtle levels of creation in the sense that you reach first I AM, then I-ness and then suddenly merge with the Self. So there is no point in pursuing a realization of I AM; it leads nowhere. The Self permeates everything and can be realized in every part of your being at any moment. The Self is your very Self right now at this very moment. You are not separate from it in time and space, nor is it something that has to be developed. It is perfect and present right here and now. You have to step out of ignorance and into Self-realization. This means stepping out of I AM and I-ness, not pursuing I AM. Pursuing I AM is a blind alley and it can go on forever; it will never take you to the Self.

6. It is true that meditation on I AM will disentangle your awareness from a number of identifications, but so will meditation on any subtle principle such as I-ness, or simply the subtlest sense of "me". Neither will give you enlightenment and in all cases you have to let go of the meditation and merge into being. This goes for all practices, not just these.

Meditation on I AM is not entirely useless, though it will not lead to Self-realization. It will disentangle awareness from a large number of identifications and this may fertilize the soul, so to speak, for Self-realization. Meditation on I-ness or the subtlest sense of "me" is equally as good as meditation on I AM. For all practices it is important to understand that in order to reach the Self one has to give up the practice at the right moment and merge into the Self.

7. No practice will ever take you there in itself. Practice is like a train ride you take to get to a destination. You have to get off at the destination or you will miss it.

No matter what kind of meditation or spiritual practice you are pursuing, you will have to give it up at the right moment in order to merge with the Self. No method will take you there by itself. If it will, it is not a method, but pure grace. Grace, however, cannot be put into practice; if it could it would not be grace. The closest one comes to putting grace into practice is to do practices to awaken and raise kundalinī. Even grace has to be surrendered to. One must surrender to the awakened kundalinī shakti and its transformative process.

8. I AM is very charming. Being in I AM is being in the now. It has power, but the power is not of the Self, it is of the subtle ego. Compared to the confused, suffering personality of common mundane consciousness, I AM seems to be freedom, and in a sense it is, but it is only temporary. If you want to get enlightened, you don't want to hunt the present moment, you want to be in that which is without now: the timeless pure being.

I AM realization is not Self-realization but realization of one's subtlest ego structures. There is a certain charm to the pure realization of I AM: one gets some present moment awareness and some liberation from the past, but it is temporary. I AM-realization feels like realizing one's essence, however, in reality one has no essence except the radical freedom of the unmanifest. Since this is unmanifest it cannot be said to be an essence, since essence implies individuality and something manifest. Self and essence are thus different and I AM-realization is not Self-realization. Since I AM-realization is situated in the present moment, it is a temporary realization and one will eventually slip out of it. The inherent power of present moment awareness is derived from I AM-ness and the illusory sense of being true to one's essence. It may dissolve numerous internal conflicts and feel liberating in that sense, but the root cause of suffering will not be undone, on the contrary one will identify more strongly with it since it will feel like one's essence. In order to get enlightened, one has to get out of this so called essence and into the timeless, unmanifest Self prior to I-ness. One reaches the Self not by holding on to the present moment or to an essence, but by radical letting go of temporality and spatiality; in other words: by letting go of the present moment and of any sense of self, and slipping into void. Once in void it is characteristic that the awareness that arises out of it will be situated in the present moment, but this awareness will be of a different quality from a relative or personal awareness that is trained to stick to the present and let go of the past. Training oneself to stick to the present will lead to I AM-ness, not to the Self. The present moment awareness of the I AM-er and the Self-realized are completely different. The I AM-er's awareness is situated in time, and thus bound, the Self-realized person's awareness is basically unmanifest and therefore non-situated with respect to time and space, yet it operates in relation to the present moment. One is bound the other is free.

9. Meditating on I AM can deconstruct some of the identifications you have with personality, but at some point it won't take you any further. At that point you have to shift your awareness to become aware of itself. Later you will have to let go of the objectification of awareness that inevitably sets in. Later still you will have to let go of observing, and simply be a witness; you may then plop into pure being. The final steps are always spiritual grace.

Meditating on I AM is, to some extent, not a waste of time as it has a certain therapeutic value. But as elaborated in the previous verse and commentary, it cannot take you to the Self, but only to your imaginary essence, and it therefore has to be given up eventually. The bridge between I AM-ness, with its associated present moment awareness, and the Self is pure awareness. So when in I AM-ness you have to let awareness become aware of itself as pure awareness, at first the awareness of awareness will not be pure, but will be colored by what is in awareness. This is what is called "objectification of awareness". When you let go of this, awareness will take on the quality of simply being a blank witness and when this blank witness witnesses itself, you have the situation previously called awareness aware of itself as pure awareness. This is the closest one can move to the Self. The final step is always grace. It is radical letting go and at the same time the Self swallowing one up. This swallowing up is grace. What is the nature of this grace? The next verse clarifies:

10. Spiritual grace is a form of kundalinī shakti or Mother Shakti. Once it awakens, love begins to control you and take over. Later you will merge. I AM and essence stand in the way of this process. You have to completely and utterly let go of anything you in any sense can be; then let go of that letting go. I AM is at the core of ignorance and it must go. When you are liberated from I AM and its counterpart, I-ness, it is called Self-realization.

Grace is divine love in action; this divine love in action resides in one as kundalinī shakti. Shakti is personified as the divine Mother. When kundalinī shakti awakens it is the Self that reaches out to you and wants to swallow you up. Of course this distinction between you and Self is illusory, but nevertheless, it is how things appear when not Self-realized. Kundalinī, when awakened, wants to remove this illusion. When asleep, kundalinī upholds the illusion. It is possible to reach the void-kind of Self-realization, without bliss, without an awakened kundalinī. But if you want the love-bliss of full realization, you will have to awaken kundalinī. The previous verse described the process of void-realization. This verse describes the transformation of a sādhana for void-realization to a sādhana of void-bliss realization - the difference being the awakened kundalinī. Next verse describes the sādhana for non-dual love-bliss realization.

11. Love-bliss is apparently dual: it can inflow from Mother or it can outflow from the Self. Ultimately the two are one. To realize this oneness is non-duality (advaita). Supreme bliss is the merging of the two flows of love without other objects than each other. This process of supreme bliss is called "god-consciousness". In god-consciousness, bliss is realized not only internally, but externally as well. The goal of god-consciousness is called "unity consciousness". In unity consciousness the Self is not only realized internally but externally as well.

Shakti personified as the divine Mother is a source of infinite love and compassion. This love and compassion can be felt as an inflow into the entire body and person at once. Simultaneously, great love for Mother flows from the Self through every pore of the body and through every part of one's person. When these two flows merge into one, it is love-bliss. The developmental phase where this merging comes about is called god-consciousness and the stable state it culminates in is called unity consciousness. In unity consciousness the Self is realized in everything exterior as well as interior, thus there is complete oneness with Mother and

Mother is realized as the Self; all is Shakti, which is the Self. This is real non-duality (advaita). Void-realization is often called non-dual, however, it is dual with respect to interior unity vs. exterior plurality; thus it is not really advaita. Also one should be aware that there are many kinds of love, which the next verse makes clear.

12 There is a kind of love associated with I AM, which is inferior since it is based in subtle ego and is dualistic. It is utilized in bhakti yoga practices such as singing bhajans, etc.

The pseudo freedom in I AM-ness should be utilized to release a sense of love for the divine as well as compassion for the person in ignorance (one "self"). It should release a strong longing for the divine in whatever form it is personified. It is, however, not the love spoken of in the previous verse as love-bliss, since this I AM-love is dualistic. I AM-love is characterized by a subtle subject, an "I", that loves an object, the source of grace, the divine. Bhakti yoga utilizes this love for the divine and transforms it into surrender. This surrender prepares for the surrender to the Self needed to attain Self-realization. Thus the dualistic surrender of bhakti has to transcend itself into unitary merging.

13. The goal of bhakti is to transcend bhakti. Hence to move from an I AM type of love to the Divine Mother love, that flows in and out at once and merges in the Self. The former love is noisy while the latter is silent. Mother is silence. When bhakti is transcended para-bhakti arises.

The goal of surrender is not surrender, but to merge into one with that to which one surrenders. This oneness can only become perfect when one merges with the Self. Supreme bhakti, or para-bhakti, arises when Mother takes over and one becomes love-bliss, as described in verse 11; bhakti then transforms from I AM-love to the god-consciousness that leads to unity consciousness. Para-bhakti is another word for supreme bliss consciousness. Bhakti is characterized by activity and longing, thus it can be called noisy. Para-bhakti on the other hand is characterized by surrender to oneness with the beloved, hence it can be called silent. In bhakti, one considers Mother to be actively reaching out for one, however, in para-bhakti one realizes Mother to be silent and forever resting in Her own nature of supreme bliss and one partakes in this bliss. Para-bhakti arises when Mother's grace has taken over one's sādhana. In regular bhakti one strives for para-bhakti to take place and take one over. In reality this taking over is the awakening of kundalinī shakti, though that may not be apparent to the bhakta. It will, however, become apparent in para-bhakti. Mother is another name for Shakti, which is the Self.

14. I AM thinks of the Self as an I-self, a "me". In reality there is no trace of "I" in the Self. I-self is subtle ego.

This verse stresses that I AM-ness is a state of personhood, a subtle state of ego, not pure being. This means that I AM-ness will have to be transcended in order to reach Self-realization. It is important that it is the I-ness of I AM that has to go away. It is not I AM as such, but identification with it; however, when identification goes away, I AM seems to break down.

15. When I AM breaks down, fear may set in because one is about to lose everything one believes oneself to be. Once free, the fear may persist without any sense of having achieved anything. Radical freedom is not limited by gains.

When I AM breaks down, it really means that one's sense of being somebody begins to disintegrate. When this disintegration sets in, fear may arise. It is a fear of death, not death of the body, but death of everything one senses oneself to be. Oddly enough, when one's self-awareness steps out of I AM and into the Self as void, there may still be fear. This fear resides in the "I", not in the Self, so one will be a witness to the fear, not a victim of the fear: one will see the "I" and its fear as something different from oneself. The "I" will also still have its wrong notion about what

193

Self-realization is, so it will still have a sense that it has not achieved its goal. This is because nothing is gained for the "I" with void Self-realization, in fact for the "I" Self-realization is solely a loss of identification and therefore a loss of substance. I AM loses I-ness and only pure being remains along with the "I" as an empty shell one now witnesses. If something was to be gained in Self-realization, Self-realization would be limited by the nature of the gain. In reality, Self-realization is radical freedom.

16. Radical freedom knows no boundaries. The Self cannot be restricted in any way. Used to being restricted within identities, stepping out of identities may cause fear. Identities react with fear when liberation arrives. At first liberation is ultimate clarity with respect to the question: Who am I? One realizes there is no answer to the question, because one is nothing. Thus getting Self-realized may be a disappointment unless there is bliss. One may even reach it and not quite know what has happened, though it will be noticed as a major change in awareness making one different from others who are not realized. For sure one will notice that I AM is an illusion.

Radical freedom is just that, because it is a state where one's self-awareness has moved from the relative to the unmanifest and has become liberated from I AM. Unmanifest knows no boundaries or restrictions, thus the Self cannot be said to be restricted in any way. As explained in the previous verse, it may give rise to fear in the mind when identification breaks down and one becomes Self-realized. Though one, when one with the Self, radically understands there is no answer to the question "Who am I?" the mind may still be confused by the question because no answer has come forth. The mind may therefore become disappointed and feel it has lost something, lost its self, and become scared. This is only a problem when one reaches blissless void-realization. When love-bliss is present, one's heart will be full and fear will go away. This is the blessing of getting realized with kundalinī shakti. Without bliss and purely in void, the only indicator of Self-realization may be an intrinsic sense of loss of personhood and of being radically different from others. One will, with time, come to understand the freedom and become attracted to sādhanas for developing love-bliss.

17. Void Self-realization is not intrinsically blissful. Bliss comes later when the Self is recognized in other.

Though love-bliss at one point will be realized as the nature of the Self, it is peculiar that the void type of Self-realization is blissless. It seems that one can step out of personhood and become liberated from I AM without quite realizing the nature of the Self.

195

Thus void-realization is really a kind of intermediate state after I-ness and prior to love-bliss. It is a shame some identify void as the highest and on a purely speculative basis reject bliss and kundalinī as mere experiences. They become stuck in an intermediary phase and misguide others. Love-bliss begins to unfold fully when one's realization of the Self begins to extend to exterior objects and other people. One begins to directly, not hypothetically or speculatively, experience other as Self. This is intrinsically blissful.

> **18. Bliss is indescribable. Symptomatically it blows the mind away and runs like a fire through the body. There is no doubt when it comes. Prior to bliss may arise supreme joy, but they are entirely different: Bliss is of the Self, supreme joy is of the mind and of I AM.**

This is the bliss associated with an awakened kundalinī shakti and which unfolds in god-consciousness as love-bliss. With an awakened kundalinī shakti it may be felt even before god-consciousness sets in as a relatively stable state; that is, even before void Self-realization has begun to be transformed to unity consciousness through god-consciousness. One should not confuse supreme joy with bliss. Bliss is a symptom of kundalinī shakti operating in the system and transforming one to be able to uphold more stable states of bliss and realization. Thus kundalinī-bliss is Mother's grace.

19. I AM refuses to go away and believes it is death to be transcended. This serves as a firewall against Self-realization. When I AM gets transcended, one will have a feeling of non-being, since there is no I AM anymore. One will lose oneself.

I AM is not an entrance to Self-realization, on the contrary it is the primal hindrance. Upon transcending I AM, the sense of being a distinct individual will go away and the mind-psyche complex may react with fear unless one is full of supreme bliss. In fact the fear may be there even while supreme bliss permeates the body. I AM is self-referential and self-perpetuating thus it is hard to transcend and hard to get rid of. When I AM is transcended one will lose the feeling of existing as an individual, thus one loses oneself to the Self. Small personhood has to be sacrificed in order to realize the Self.

20. When losing oneself, fear may arise in the mind. I AM instinctively knows this and fights against Self-realization by suggesting I AM is the highest. When one transcends I AM the great void arises. This void is the Self devoid of bliss. Bliss comes later.

As explained in the previous verse, fear accompanies progressive loss of personhood. When personhood is fully lost one abides in the Self, or rather, when one abides in the Self, personhood is transcended. Some personhood remains after Self-realization, but all and any identification with it has ceased. Since primary Self-realization is characterized by absence of ignorance, it is called void. There is of course presence of Self-realization, but there is nothing to qualify the realization at all, hence it is called void.

21. Void is indescribable. It can only be described negatively as absence of I AM, or as radical freedom from I-ness.

Absence of any qualification can only be called "void", thus it is indescribable and can only be hinted at with negative terms such as absence of any sense of personhood, including I-ness and I AM. With the term "radical freedom" is meant absolute freedom from any qualifying I-ness; there simply is no sense of I in the radical freedom of the Self.

22. There is no one to be called the Self. The Self is not even no-one; it simply IS. I AM is the most subtle subjective self distinguished simply by being definable as an individual entity. Individuality is not relevant in the Self.

The Self is void and hence there is no qualifying sense of personhood in the Self. Thus there is no longer any sense of being a subject; no longer any I-ness. However, even this is inadequate when describing the Self, for the Self is one's very Self as pure being. This is interesting in relation to the subtle sense of I AM, since this I AM-ness is the most subtle sense of personhood, of being a subject, that exists. Thus I AM can be said to be the essence of one's subject, of one's personhood, but it cannot be said to be the Self since it hides the Self and makes it inaccessible for normal awareness. The Self knows no sense of individuality.

23. Nothing is relevant in the Self apart from pure being, pure awareness and supreme bliss. All three should be realized for it to be called enlightenment. In basic void Self-realization one has merely realized the Self as pure being.

The Self has three qualities: being, awareness and bliss. However, these three are not qualities as such but are the inherent nature of the One which is called the Self. In voidness there is only the sense of pure being, bliss has not yet unfolded.

24. Meditation on supreme bliss can lead to Self-realization and full enlightenment.

One can experience bliss prior to Self-realization if one's kundalinī is awakened and active. Meditation on this bliss, meaning becoming fully saturated by it and ultimately dissolving one's awareness in it, will lead to Self-realization. In fact it will lead beyond basic void Self-realization to god-consciousness and unity-consciousness as it transforms itself along the way.

25. Meditation on pure being and pure awareness can lead to Self-realization.

Meditation on pure being and pure awareness in and of itself can lead to void Self-realization. Unless kundalinī is awakened and bliss pours into one, it will not lead to god-consciousness and unity consciousness.

26. For bliss to come kundalinī must awaken and rise. Hence without an awakened kundalinī one cannot meditate on supreme bliss as a path to enlightenment. On the other hand, when kundalinī awakens, one will be meditated on spontaneously by Shakti. Unless Shakti begins to meditate on one throughout the day, one cannot say one's kundalinī has awakened.

Here the main features of an awakened kundalinī are explained. First of all one will have the peculiar experience that one becomes the object of Shakti's meditation and that one is becoming transformed by it. Also it is noteworthy that this meditation of Shakti's goes on throughout the day, not just when one sits for meditation. Once Shakti begins to meditate one, one does not have to do much to keep the process going except surrender to Shakti. Kundalinī kriyā, kundalinī-prāṇāyāma and chakra kriyā will help keep the process going. One way to surrender to Shakti is to meditate on supreme bliss since bliss and Shakti are inseparable.

27. Kundalinī may for various reasons rise without being awakened. This may temporarily give some disturbance or some bliss. One should seize the moment and meditate to fully awaken kundalinī.

Temporary arousals of kundalini may occur. These are not to be confused with an awakened kundalinī. An awakened kundalinī does not necessarily arise in any dramatic way. Temporary kundalinī arousals will give rise to bliss. They are beneficial and inspiring, though some may out of ignorance and incomprehension react to them with fear. Do not be afraid; seize the opportunity and pray to kundalinī to awaken fully. Surrender to Shakti.

28. Without kundalinī, enlightenment will never be full. Shiva needs Shakti; pure being needs supreme bliss to unfold and bless the world. Shakti is the transformative power of the Self. Without Shakti, Self-realization is internal only and one will not be able to awaken the spirituality of others; one will merely be able to lecture.

Shiva is pure being and Shakti is the dynamic force of pure being; they are one and inseparable, though to the uninitiated they appear as two. Void Self-realization can be said to be realization of the pure being aspect, or Shiva aspect, of the Self. Full enlightenment requires full realization of Shakti as well as Shiva, and this realization develops during god-consciousness and matures in unity consciousness. Once one has to some degree realized the Shakti aspect of pure being, one becomes contagious and the kundalinī of others may awaken simply by being in one's company or meditating with one; this is a low level of shaktipāt.

29. Shaktipāt is the transformative power of the Self (which is Shakti) applied for the benefit of Self-realization and enlightenment of others. Thus enlightenment that transcends I AM and sees the Self in other is entirely unselfish. Shaktipāt is grace.

Shaktipāt is the peculiar phenomenon that the fully awakened kundalinī of one who is also Self-realized may awaken the kundalinī of another. With practice, one may control this awakening and give it as an initiation, it may also occur spontaneously.

30. Giving shaktipāt is not possible while stuck in I AM. As soon as the Self is fully realized as pure being and Shakti, one may begin to give mild degrees of shaktipāt spontaneously. This is because shaktipāt is of the Self prior to I AM and in no way follows the command of the ego. Shaktipāt is given solely by and from Shakti. If Shakti has taken one over and meditates on one completely, then others may accidentally receive shaktipāt by meditating in one's vicinity. As such shaktipāt is pure grace.

Shaktipāt cannot be given by those who merely are in I AM or are in void Self-realization. One has to have an awakened kundalinī and surrendered to kundalinī so that Shakti meditates on one completely. This surrender is paramount. It is not the personhood who gives shaktipāt, but Shakti of her own accord. By having surrendered to Shakti, one may become a conduit for shaktipāt to happen. So much so that one may eventually begin to be able to turn it on at will. But initially it will be a spontaneous thing that happens for one, rather than something one can initiate by will.

31. Grace means one receives a spiritual blessing without having earned or deserved it. Grace is the nature of Shakti, of Mother. Adore Mother.

Mother Divine is a personification of Shakti; Shakti is Mother, they cannot be distinguished. Shakti is not a dumb force, it is pure being in action. Shaktipāt happens by itself and comes to those who are ready for it; as such it is grace. One cannot earn a right to shaktipāt by certain deeds, but one can prepare oneself by practices such as kundalinī prānāyāma and kundalinī kriyā that invite one to surrender to Shakti.

32. Mother is the unity of Shiva and Shakti. Shakti is the mother of supreme bliss, the mother of enlightenment, the mother of shaktipāt. Mother is Shakti and She is one with Shiva. Adore Mother.

Though Shakti is called "Mother", Mother called "Shakti", Mother Shakti is one with Shiva; there is no duality between Shiva and Shakti. Shakti is the giver of bliss, enlightenment and shaktipāt as well as the upholder of ignorance. It is in the power of Mother to keep one in ignorance as well as to take one out of it and into the supreme bliss of full enlightenment. It is easier to think of Shakti as Mother, rather than as the radical energy of pure being, and as such Shakti is to be adored. Mother is the giver of grace. Mother is grace.

> **33. Mother does not have a form nor is She a separate entity. Think of the most extreme, detached, supreme love and you are thinking of Mother. Think of the grace that picks up the most broken man and gives him enlightenment, then you are thinking of Mother. Think of nothing but infinite blue consciousness made out of supreme bliss, and you are thinking of Mother. Mother is everything and nothing at the same time. She is you and I prior to I AM. Thus when She gives shaktipāt from one to another, She is merely dancing with Herself. Mother is mysterious. Adore Mother.**

"Infinite blue consciousness" is not a metaphor. In meditation the blue, infinite space of pure being can be experienced directly. This blue is Shakti and Shiva as one and it is the Self.

> **34. Surrendering to supreme bliss is surrendering to the Self and is surrendering to Mother. Surrender should know no result or benefit; it should simply BE.**

Surrender is the natural state of the Self. By practicing surrender to Mother, one practices Self-realization. This is para-bhakti.

Bhakti yoga is dualistic devotion to God; para-bhakta is monistic surrender to one's very Self mediated by Mother.

35. Regular bhakti is from I AM. Para-bhakti is surrendering to being meditated on by Mother.

The dualism of bhakti yoga stems from the fact that it develops and deepens the relationship between the personhood and the Godhead; there is an "I" in relation to God; hence bhakti does not transcend I AM. When I AM is transcended, bhakti is transcended and becomes para-bhakti. Para-bhakti differs from bhakti in that in bhakti you meditate on God, while in para-bhakti, God meditates on you and you practice surrender to this meditation of Gods.

36. Surrender to Mother that She may meditate you out of I AM and into enlightenment.

Why is para-bhakti desirable? Because it is the process that takes one out of I AM and into the Self.

37. Surrender to Mother that the Self may swallow you up.

Mother is grace. Grace is when Mother actively works for one's liberation; in other words meditates on one. Surrendering to Mother is to surrender to this process of grace; its goal is to become one with the Self, which is one with Mother.

38. Surrender to Mother that She may burn you in the fire of love-bliss.

Grace is felt as love-bliss. Love-bliss is like a fire that burns away one's ignorance.

39. Love-bliss is the nature of the Self. Mother may infuse you with it prior to your enlightenment. Such is Mother's grace.

Furthermore, love-bliss is not only how grace is felt, it is the nature of the Self. It is remarkable that one may become infused with love-bliss even prior to one's full enlightenment; this is grace.

40. Grace is the nature of the enlightened Self, in void there is no grace. While enlightenment is highly desirable, Self-realization as void is inferior. However, many, not knowing full enlightenment as grace, call void full enlightenment. Both are free from I AM and both are stable states.

It is an interesting distinction between the void Self-realization and god-consciousness that there is no grace in void Self-realization. Void Self-realization is desirable, but it is far from the highest state of enlightenment.

41. Full enlightenment wants to be shared, void does not care.

One characteristic distinction between full enlightenment and void is that void is empty and does not know love-bliss or shaktipāt. Shaktipāt is the inherent nature of full enlightenment wanting to be shared. Void does not have such an inherent urge to be shared. Void is utterly detached and considers such as love-bliss and shaktipāt to be mere experiences in the relative sphere and hence illusory and to be avoided. Pity on them!

42. I AM is subtle ego, worthy of neither being called enlightenment nor Self-realization. It is a subtle state of mind characterized by being the self-referential power of I-ness. Thus when "I" arises, it immediately claims to be; or I-ness says "I AM". Out of this all ignorance arises.

A step further away from full enlightenment, you have the I AM type of realization. I AM is characterized by a self-referential awareness of individual being, and as such it may resemble the way enlightenment is described, but I AM-ness is in no way Self-realization or enlightenment. I AM is the basis of ignorance.

43. To become free of I AM, you have to transcend I-ness. I-ness is transcended by grace; or by awareness becoming aware of itself as pure being; or by merging with supreme bliss; or by kundalinī.

I-ness is the basis and essence of I AM. "I" refers to itself and considers that it is; thus I AM arises. In order to reach the Self one has to transcend I AM and I-ness. The means are grace, Self-awareness of awareness, bliss and kundalinī.

44. Kundalinī is individualized Shakti, as such kundalinī holds the structure of your ignorance as well as your liberation.

Kundalinī is not an impersonal, universal force; it is the creative force behind the individualized structure of your entire ignorant being. As such, kundalinī holds the key to your ignorance as well as your liberation. When kundalinī upholds ignorance it is said to be asleep, when it acts as grace and transforms you towards enlightenment, kundalinī is said to be awakened. Kundalinī is individualized Shakti.

45. Supreme bliss comes when kundalinī reaches the brain. Awareness becomes aware of itself when kundalinī reaches the brain. Kundalinī is the grace that dissolves I-ness. There is no aspect of enlightenment that is not given by kundalinī.

Kundalinī gives all the four means of enlightenment mentioned in verse 43. All the four means are aspects of Shakti and kundalinī is one with Shakti.

46. Kundalinī skips the stage of pure void by giving bliss. When kundalinī gives Self-realization; it will be

with a flowering seed of full enlightenment. Others who reach the void without an awakened kundalinī do not have this flowering seed, and will think there is nothing more to enlightenment then what they have themselves reached.

As mentioned in verse 40, void-realizers tend to think they have reached the highest; however, they have not. Kundalinī will give full enlightenment to void-realizers as well as to others. By itself, kundalinī will simply skip the void Self-realization stage and take one directly to god-consciousness.

47. Void-realizers tend to denigrate kundalinī as a mere experience; not knowing what they are talking about. Thus their teachings lure others away from Mother's grace.

48. I AM-realizers don't even understand void. They denigrate kundalinī and claim their realization is void. Thus their teachings lure others away from Mother's grace.

Mother's grace is alpha and omega if one wants the full enlightenment of unity consciousness. Void and I AM are kinds of traps in that those in those states tend to overestimate their own levels of realization and denigrate others.

49. Teachings that do not deconstruct themselves are not pertinent to void Self-realization. Teachings that do not aid in surrendering to Mother Shakti are not pertinent to unity consciousness.

Interestingly, two types of teachings lead to the two different states of realization known as void and unity consciousness. If one simply wants void, surrendering to Mother Shakti is not relevant, but one should engage in teachings that deconstruct themselves. If the teachings do not deconstruct themselves, they will bind the mind in given conclusions, and at best fixate one in I AM. Mother Shakti is you - is kundalinī and surrendering to it means getting it awakened through shaktipāt and surrendering to kundalinī's operations in you after that.

50. Neither void Self-realization nor full enlightenment can be taught, but pointers can be given. Most teachings point in the wrong direction since they point at I AM.

A clear understanding of the trap of I AM is helpful on the path to void Self-realization and enlightenment. This is because such teachings will deconstruct themselves and point to either void or god-consciousness or unity consciousness. Void can of course not be taught, since it is void. God-consciousness and unity consciousness, being beyond basic void-consciousness, can likewise not be taught.

51. Surrendering to Mother means merging with Shakti. Merging with Shakti ultimately means merging with Shiva. When I AM dissolves and you realize your oneness with Shiva, you are free in void Self-realization. Merge Shiva and Shakti and you are free in unity consciousness.

Shiva and Shakti are one; yet they represent two aspects of the Self that can be realized independently. Thus Shiva can be realized as void Self-realization. Shakti can be realized as bliss consciousness. Ultimately, though, the unity of Shiva and Shakti will have to be realized in unity consciousness.

52. In fact there is nothing to be free of. You are getting rid of ignorance which is getting rid of what you haven't got. Pure being has never been anything but pure, only you as ignorant don't know it and don't live it because you live from I AM and the ego that builds upon it.

It is interesting that pure being is eternally pure and has never been anything but pure. This means that getting Self-realized is not a question of purifying or evolving the Self; it is solely a question of getting rid of the illusion that we are not already the Self. In other words, we have to get rid of what we do not have: ignorance. It is a paradoxical situation: on the one hand we are the Self, eternally pure and free, yet we do not know it because of ignorance. The reason we do not know it is because of I AM and the ego that builds upon it; in other words, because we identify with the fluctuations of consciousness. As long as there are notions like "I am this and I am that" we have a hindrance to Self-realization. One should contemplate that one is nothing.

53. Awareness in and of itself is one with pure being. As soon as there is an object of awareness, there is I AM. Let awareness become aware of itself, and the Self prior to I AM will reveal itself.

When the object appears in the ignorant mind, the notion that one is either separate from it or identical with it will arise; in either case the sense of being an individual and qualified entity arises; this sense is I AM. I AM arises out of I-ness as soon as there is an object in one's ignorant awareness; this does not happen after Self-realization. One should contemplate the pure nature of one's awareness. Pure awareness is prior to I AM so when awareness becomes aware of itself in its purity, one will become aware of the Self.

54. Objects of awareness are constructs of consciousness. They do not have reality in and of themselves, but seem to have as I AM is projected onto them and they acquire a status of being.

What status do the objects of awareness have if they are capable of distracting one from the Self? As soon as one acquires a self-referential identity with I AM, the objects acquire their own self-referential identity. This tendency stops with Self-realization. In reality objects of awareness are nothing but constructs of consciousness without any substantial reality of their own.

55. The world appears on the screen of pure being.

In one sense the world appears on the screen of pure being because the world is known only as objects of awareness. In another sense, it is realized in god-consciousness that outer objects are also manifest out of pure being; thus everything is realized as Shakti and literally as appearances in and out of pure being (Shakti).

56. Awareness can become aware of itself between objects of awareness and behind objects of awareness. This instruction is deceptively simple but hard to put to practice. It is better to surrender to Mother if you have her grace.

The pure awareness of pure being can become self-aware between objects and behind objects, but not in or as objects. It sounds easy enough that all one has to do to get Self-realized is to put one's awareness on the gaps between thoughts, but it is not quite so simple. The reason it is not so simple, is that I-ness has to go away for one to become Self-realized. Awareness has to become aware of itself prior to I-ness and independently of objects of awareness. Why does the verse say it is better to surrender to Mother's grace rather than practice awareness becoming aware of itself? Because the step of transcending I-ness cannot be performed by anything possessed by I-ness; it can only be transcended if the Self spontaneously pulls awareness back into itself. This pull is grace, it is Shakti in action; Mother's grace. This pull back into the Self is Shakti pulling her manifestation back into its source; in other words, granting Self-realization.

57. Mother's grace is omnipresent. Awaken it with shaktipāt. Invoke it through kundalinī prāṇāyāma and kundalinī kriyā meditation.

Where can one find Mother's grace? Mother's grace is omnipresent and can be invoked through some simple practices. Two such practices are kundalinī prāṇāyāma and kundalinī kriyā meditation. Grace can first and foremost be awakened by shaktipāt. What is the difference between invoking grace and awakening grace? When you invoke it, it is temporary. When awakened it will be a permanent situation. After awakening grace you can invoke it.

> **58. Kundalinī prāṇāyāma: Breathe in to the count of three. Hold your breath to the count of three. Breathe out to the count of three. This is one round. Do as many rounds as you please. Instead of counting one could mentally repeat the mantra "om aim hrim klim" or some other mantra. While breathing in, visualize and sense kundalinī-shakti rising up the spine. While holding the breath and while breathing out, visualize and sense kundalinī-shakti radiating from the brain in all directions. Keep an easy, relaxed pace.**

Initially, much Shakti will build up in the brain with this practice, but after a while it will build up in the entire body. It will clear the passage for kundalini from the root to the brain and will open the chakra of the brain (sahasrāra). If counting to 2 or 4 works better, do that. The important thing is to have an equal duration for all three phases of breathing. The mantra is not important. The important thing is the visualization and the sense that shakti moves up the spine and radiates from the brain. Make sure to have a relaxed duration of counting so you can easily do this wonderful prānāyāma without interruption for half an hour or more.

59. Kundalinī kriyā meditation: Three meditations. 1. Follow the breath; on the in-breath sense you expand beyond the limits of the physical body, on the out-breath let go and merge. 2. Follow the breath; on the in-breath sense energy rise from the perineum up the spine and into the brain. On the out-breath sense energy radiate from the brain in all directions. 3. Simultaneously sense Shakti enter the entire spine from all directions and radiate from the spine in all direction.

This is a wonderful practice. Do it once or twice daily for 50 minutes and you will soon see results. When doing part 3 you will experience the spine become very hot. This is as it should be. You can visualize it as a white hot rod being heated from the outside and radiating heat from the inside.

60. Chakra prānāyāma: Focus on a chakra. Sense energy moving forwards on the in-breath, then

backwards on the out-breath. Do this six to ten times. Then sense a ball of energy expand in the chakra on the in-breath and contract on the out-breath. Do this six to ten times. Then sense energy radiate from the chakra on both the in-breath and out-breath. Do this six to ten times. This is one round. Do one round in each chakra from the bottom up and down again. Move energy up and down when shifting from one chakra to the next.

61. Inner light arises when I AM is transcended and kundalinī to some degree operates in the brain. Then bliss also arises.

Inner light and bliss may arise of its own accord during meditation; meditate on this inner light and bliss.

62. Bliss arises when I AM is transcended and kundalinī to some degree operates in the heart; more intense bliss arises as kundalinī moves above the heart. Supreme bliss arises when kundalinī enters the brain.

There are various kinds of bliss. They are all beneficial to Self-realization and can be used to meditate on.

63. Liberation from I AM is rather sudden. At one point it is simply not there anymore. When approaching this shift, it may generate fear in the mind that one is about to lose one's self, which is quite true. However, one will gain the Self.

One should not be too alarmed when fear or disquiet sets in. It is quite natural yet quite groundless. One is about to realize one's real Self and get out of identification with an illusory self. The illusory self will fight for its survival and one of its means of fighting is to generate fear and disquiet.

64. As nothingness becomes more and more real to you, meaninglessness will set in. Do not be alarmed by this, but develop equanimity and compassion.

Pure void Self-realization is not a particularly nice state, though it is freedom.

65. Similarly depression may set in as one realizes that all identities and pleasures are mere figments of imagination. Develop surrendering to Shakti, Mother's grace.

It is important to develop bhakti and para-bhakti to Mother's grace, to Shakti. Shakti bhakti will help one get through the depression that may set in when one begins to realize that everything is void.

66. Mother's grace is the boat that takes one across the sea of ignorance and pain.

Surrender to Mother's grace. Do the above mentioned practices and develop a sense of Mother's grace. Then when you find it, surrender to it completely.

67. When Mother's grace grabs you, you will never be lost again; grace will take you to the very end of sādhana. Sādhana will become spontaneous and odd movements and actions may set in during meditation; these are known as kriyās. Do not be alarmed by any of this, but surrender to Shakti.

When the Shakti grabs you, kriyās may set in. Kriyās are spontaneous movements, utterances, visions or inspirations that may come during meditation. One's arms may twitch, or one may bend the body or rotate it back and forth along the spine, just to mention a few common kriyās. Some utter meaningless sounds and others assume various postures or hand gestures.

68. Mother's grace is love. Surrender to Mother.

No matter how dramatic one's kriyās may be, one should remember they are Mother's grace purifying one's system so it may uphold Self-realization and enlightenment. Such grace is love and is to be surrendered to.

69. Do not desire void. Void is devoid of grace. Surrender to Mother instead of to void.

The sādhana of surrendering to Shakti will lead to not only Self-realization, but also to god-consciousness and unity consciousness. With Mother's grace in the form of Shakti having grabbed one, there is no point in desiring void Self-realization.

70. Desiring the Self will not lead to the Self. Such desire must be given up also. Surrender to Mother.

It is a common misunderstanding that the more one desires the Self, the more one deserves to find it. It is not so. All desires must be transcended including the desire for liberation. Usually such desires do not go away and they may even persist after liberation, but one should definitely transcend them so awareness may rest in itself and one may realize pure being. Once Shakti awakens in one and grabs one, one should surrender to it.

71. While meditating on silence, bliss may arise. Remain in the bliss, but do not lose the silence or else you will become lost in ecstasy. Ecstasy is on the level of I AM. Silent, still bliss is of the Self. One has to go through ecstasy to reach the supreme silent bliss. Do not get stuck in ecstasy, but on the other hand do not dismiss ecstasy. Welcome ecstasy and pass through it to the Self.

Ecstasy is a doorway to bliss; bliss is a doorway to the Self. In the beginning little bliss may arise, then ecstasy and with the ecstasy so much disturbance that one loses the meditation altogether. It is important to remain calm during ecstasy in order that one may transcend it and reach the supreme bliss of the Self, which is silent.

72. Living in the world while silent inside is like listening to a symphony where every instrument is out of tune. Develop compassion for others and pray they may become silent also.

Void Self-realization comes with its own problems. As you become pure inside, you begin to sense how impure others are. The solution is to develop compassion and to move on from void to bliss.

> **73. Living in the world while blissful inside is like being hopelessly in love. You transform people you pass without anyone ever knowing. Develop compassion and equanimity.**

Bliss consciousness also comes with its own problems and blessings. When Shakti has grabbed you, you become contagious, and even people you sit in a room with while listening to a lecture may get grabbed by your Shakti and receive spontaneous shaktipāt. One should develop compassion and equanimity.

> **74. Mother plays hide and seek with her devotees. Do not be disturbed by this. When Mother is hiding, surrender to void and silence while keeping up your practice of kundalinī prānāyāma and kundalinī kriyā. Then Mother will reveal herself shortly.**

The presence of Shakti and the degree to which it grabs one will go up and down, but this is quite normal and there is no reason to be alarmed when it is low. When bliss is low, one should surrender to void, or, if Self-realized, simply rest in silent presence. It is important to keep up one's spiritual practices when Shakti is low, because that way Shakti will soon grab one fully again.

75. These tribulations are incomprehensible to those who are I AM realizers. Yet they are signs of advanced spirituality and well progressing sādhana.

One should not be discouraged by other's lack of understanding. It is important to have trust in Shakti and the process of shaktipāt, and also trust in one's practices. Otherwise those of different realization than what one is aiming for, may discourage one and make one leave one's path and settle for something inferior.

76. I AM realizers are satisfied with their realization and happy about their gains and accomplishments. Such notions are entirely absent in the Self.

One should not compare one's sense of achievement with that of those on inferior paths. In fact one should realize that all such notions are absent in and above void Self-realization. They are signs of I AM and result from I AM.

77. The Self knows no Self-satisfaction, no pride and no sense of accomplishment. Meditate on the absence of these notions.

If assailed by pride of one's accomplishments, etc., one should meditate on the absence of these in the Self.

78. Meditate on void when disturbed by I AM. When moving out of I AM, meditate on Mother and surrender to grace.

Similarly, when inferior realization disturbs one, like if one feels tempted to settle for less than the Self and remain in I AM-ness, one should either meditate on void or meditate on Shakti and surrender to Shakti.

79. The Self is one with grace and one with Mother. Ultimately this will be realized; meanwhile grace seems to originate from a transcendental source best called Mother, but any name could do. Once unity is realized, this apparent duality between the Self and Mother may affectionately remain as a play.

"Mother" is really a metaphorical name for the divine intelligence inherent in grace. This divine intelligence is rather incomprehensible even to the wise; hence devotion to it will remain even after unity has been achieved.

80. The small self does not vanish or dissolve; it is just not you anymore. Thus you become a witness to your former personality in all its levels of manifestation.

It is a common misunderstanding that the small self disappears with Self-realization, but in reality it does not. What does vanish, though, is identification with it. For identification to vanish, you have to get rid of I-ness. I-ness is the identification mechanism prior to, and responsible for, I AM. Once you have rid yourself of I-ness, you will become a witness to your former self. If the small self vanished entirely, you would become like a vegetable, unable to act or respond to your name and you would not know your history.

81. The witness consciousness characterizes the Self-realized state.

This witness consciousness, where you witness your former self from the unmanifest pure being, is a major characteristic of the Self-realized state.

82. The unitary consciousness characterizes full enlightenment, or unity consciousness.

Unity consciousness is characterized by seeing the Self in everything.

83. In between you live in a phase of waxing and waning love-bliss.

God-consciousness is not a stable state like void Self-realization is, it is an intermediary state between void Self-realization and unity consciousness that goes up and down in intensity. Some days there is no bliss; then there may be a week of massive bliss, then a few days of no bliss, etc.

84. I AM is characterized by a sense of being prior to personality. However, it is not freedom like in the witnessing state; it is a sense of being present here and now detached from the history of the personality.

I AM realizers may recognize some of the descriptions of void Self-realization and erroneously conclude that they have reached Self-realization. One such similarity may lie in the sense of being in the now.

> **85. Pain only exists in the present moment, just as everything else. However, I AM is characterized by a sense of detachment from pain. The pain may remain, but one senses oneself as not caught up in it as if pain belonged to the past. Thus one may confuse the I AM stance of detachment from personality with witnessing, but they are not the same. Witnessing is radical freedom, not detached observation from a peripheral stance.**

One should understand about being in the present that nothing exists outside the present moment. There is a popular understanding that the present moment somehow is a doorway to liberation from pain, suffering and ignorance. This is sadly not so, but present moment awareness is a doorway to I AM-ness. When in I AM, one may feel liberated from pain and suffering, but in reality one has only become detached from it by resting in the ultimate source of pain and suffering. The source of pain is of course slightly prior to pain so resting in the source will feel like liberation or witnessing. It is, however, not what is meant with witnessing when describing Self-realization.

86. In reality I AM is in itself the source of pain. It is the producer of pain, while the mind is the container of pain.

Because of I AM pain arises in the mind. Once a situation arises in life that contradicts or counteracts one's sense of who one is, one's I AM-ness, then pain arises. Such pain will not arise for the Self-realized. Pain may arise in the mind if life becomes challenging, even for the Self-realized, but the Self-realized will not have any identification with it, while the I AM'er will identify with it and feel threatened. The Self-realized does not feel threatened by pain.

87. The Self knows neither pleasure nor pain. It is intrinsically blissful awareness. It can be aware of pain felt in the body or mind, but it is never contaminated by it.

Why does the Self-realized not feel threatened by pain? Because pain only exists in the mind and only threatens I AM; both of which have been transcended. The Self in and of itself can be either void or blissful. It can be aware of pain, of course, but the pain will remain in levels of consciousness above I AM, and never contaminate the Self. This does not mean that a Self-realized person cannot suffer as much as anybody else, but he will not be identified with the sufferer.

88. Freedom means being untouched by pleasure or pain while remaining fully aware of such.

This freedom is only possible in, at least, Self-realization. Similarly as with pain, pleasure will not touch the Self.

89. The Self remains void or bliss, despite the presence of pleasure or pain.

The reason for this freedom is the fact that the Self does not identify with whatever may be going on in the mind or emotions, whether painful or pleasurable. Depending on one's level of realization, the Self will be void or bliss. The presence of bliss or void is not dependent on the presence of pleasure or pain.

90. Since the Self can be aware of pleasure and pain, yet remains untainted thereby, the realized one may either live as a recluse or as one fully engaged in life seemingly subject to pleasure and pain.

One cannot judge the level of realization on the way a person lives his life or behaves.

91. Life is intrinsically enjoyable to the enlightened one.

Come pleasure or pain, there will be a certain enjoyment since all is seen as the Self. This grows as realization deepens from void Self-realization, through bliss consciousness to unity consciousness.

92. Void permeates everything. Thus peace is omnipresent.

This may not yet be realized in void Self-realization, but it will become obvious during god consciousness and in unity consciousness.

93. Bliss permeates everything. Thus Shakti is omnipresent.

This becomes obvious during god consciousness. Shakti is bliss; one cannot distinguish the two.

94. In love with Shakti one loves everything. Bliss thereby acquires an unselfish stance unknown to those who are not in god-consciousness or unity-consciousness.

The bliss of god-consciousness is different from the bliss experienced in ecstatic moments of meditation. It is calm and serene and utterly detached from anything; it has no source or reason, it simply is.

95. In unity consciousness the joy and suffering of others is seen as a play of consciousness.

Joy and suffering is seen as a play of consciousness, it does not hold the reality it used to in lesser states of consciousness. Everything arises out of Shakti (Mother). Perceiving suffering as Mother's suffering generates enormous compassion, yet you are detached and perceive the sufferer and the suffering as a play of divine bliss, which is the Self (Shiva-Shakti).

96. In god-consciousness the suffering of others registers as a disturbance in Shakti. Hence unity has to be developed.

Suffering is seen as a disturbance in Shakti. On the one hand one sees bliss, yet one sees the sufferer and the suffering. In this state compassion is filled with bliss. One sees the sufferer and the suffering, but one simultaneously sees it as divine grace in operation.

97. In void-consciousness the suffering of others registers as an unreal overlay on void. Hence one needs to awaken Shakti.

Suffering is seen as an illusion; just like everything else. In pure Self-realization everything is seen as void, even the suffering of others, which is true enough, but it lacks compassion. Recognizing the other as Shakti and the suffering as Shakti generates compassion since you begin to see your Self in the other.

98. In I AM the suffering of others registers as their own error. Hence compassion needs to be developed.

Suffering is seen as error on behalf of the sufferer.

99. Throughout suffering remains an illusion, just as pleasure. It is experienced as real by the mind and body,

but nevertheless as unreal. When you transcend the mind and body, you transcend pleasure and pain even though the experience of them will continue to be witnessed.

Throughout the various levels of consciousness suffering is seen as unreal; so is pleasure. It is cognized that suffering exists only in the mind, and the status ascribed to the mind in the various states of consciousness will be the status ascribed to suffering.

100. When pleasure and pain are seen as Shakti, one realizes everything is beloved Mother and unity arises.

Supreme devotion is not disturbed by the experience of pain, on the contrary: when pleasure and pain are seen as Shakti, one realizes everything is Mother's grace and one surrenders the more to Mother Shakti.

101. Then freedom from pleasure and pain arises. Only then can one speak of being in non-duality.

Non-duality arises simultaneously with freedom from pleasure and pain. "Only then" refers to the previous verse where the criteria is seeing everything as Shakti. When everything is seen as

Shakti, you have transcended pleasure and pain, though pleasure and pain will continue to exist for your mind and body. But they will not be you and you will be free.

102. Non- duality means the Self recognizes the Self in other, animate or inanimate. This is supremely blissful. Everything is seen as Mother.

Not until everything is seen as Mother Shakti can one say one is in non-duality. In non-duality one sees the Self in and as everything. Thus the Self and Mother are one. Immature neo-Advaita style non-duality is merely an internal non-duality where awareness rests in non-dual pure being, but there is still duality between inner and outer and between the various outer objects, including the mind and the emotions.

103. Mother encompasses everything with love and compassion. Even suffering and pain.

Seeing everything as one includes seeing everything with the eye of compassion and love. This has nothing to do with what may go on in the mind, but solely speaks of what goes on in the Self – where nothing really goes on, but out of which things flow; and in this case one thing that may flow is compassion.

104. Mother is felt as vibrant Shakti in the beginning, later as moments of bliss, later as pure Shakti permeating every cell of the body as massive bliss. This bliss is contagious, thus Mother is compassion.

This describes the progressive growth of how one relates to Mother Shakti. Ultimately shaktipāt will happen spontaneously from oneself to others and the bliss will be contagious. It is important that there are two preparatory stages where there is first bliss, or what we could better describe as ecstasy, which is bliss and agitation mixed together, then one that is silent, then one that is full of bliss again, but this time of lovebliss, which is supreme bliss and love fused with utter silence and stillness.

105. Compassion is the natural state. I-ness disturbs this by introducing I AM.

I AM is the killer of compassion and the killer of non-duality. I AM is the first ignorance and defines the border between the enlightened state and the ignorant state. You are no more enlightened if you are in I AM than if you are in the ego and its desires and aversions. It is a myth that I AM is sacred. I AM is the mother of ignorance.

106. I-ness and duality arise at the same moment. They are inseparable. Non-duality (advaita) is only possible when I-ness is transcended.

One has to transcend I-ness in order to have any hope of ever reaching the true non-dual (advaitic) state. Once I-ness is transcended, internal non-duality will become a reality, but one will still see duality with respect to outer objects. Only in unity consciousness is non-duality a full reality.

107. Internal non-duality is a reality in void consciousness; however it is marked by duality between internal and external, where external is seen as an empty plurality; hence, since it is empty, it is imagined to be non-dual and advaitic. However, external non-duality only becomes a reality with god-consciousness and flowers to its fullness in unity consciousness.

Void consciousness is the same as basic Self-realization. In the first stage of enlightenment, which is basic Self-realization, one thinks that the internal non-duality encompasses outer objects also, but it does not. The inner non-duality of Self-realization comes about by being one with void and the unmanifest. There is of course no duality in unmanifest void, so it is easy to claim it is having realized the epitome of advaita. However, one has not

238

realized oneness with everything outer. Perhaps as a mood of oneness with everybody and everything, but real and complete non-duality is an explosion of Shakti in and as everything outer and inner.

108. Internal non-duality means there is no plurality in one's self-understanding. This is only possible in, at least, void consciousness where I-ness is transcended and there is no longer any self-referential aspect to one's self-understanding.

This state demands that one's awareness has gone beyond I AM and has lost any sense of I AM-ness. I AM is the death of searching because it is so easy to get stuck there. Once one transcends I AM and the vibratory sense of I (the I-ness) that lies just prior to that, one arrives at the Self and becomes Self-realized. I-ness is so subtle it has no qualities other than being self-referential, and is merely felt as a vibration or a vague sense of "me".

109. Internal non-duality is still marked by duality between inside and outside; thus the Self is not seen in external objects. External objects appear empty and meaningless.

Freedom from identification ultimately is Self-realization. In Self-realization you have transcended basic I-ness and merged your awareness into unmanifest void. Voidness is also what you see around you but not as a fullness, rather as an emptiness and an utter lack of content, value and meaning. It is easy to fool oneself and imagine this is the non-dual state, but it is not, it is merely the voidness of Self-realization projected onto everything, not full enlightenment understood as unity consciousness.

110. Void-consciousness only acquires meaning when external objects are begun to be seen as vibrant Shakti; then supreme bliss arises and one enters god-consciousness.

In order to move from the pure voidness of Self-realization, you have to get your inner Shakti activated. This inner Shakti lies within you as kundalinī. To get kundalinī awakened, you either have to pursue appropriate sādhana diligently for months or years or be blessed with shaktipāt from a competent master. Once the inner Shakti is awakened and one has surrendered to it as appropriate, then after some months or years one will begin to see this Shakti in everything as Mother's grace. This is the dawning of unity consciousness and is in itself known as god-consciousness. God-consciousness can last for years and be a fairly stable state in itself, though it is usually unstable and one fluctuates between void, bliss and unity, as the next verse explains.

111. God consciousness is not a stable state; thus one goes in and out of bliss. If one is stable in void Self-realization, going in and out of bliss is the same as internal non-duality temporarily becoming external also.

The internal non-duality of void consciousness can merge into god consciousness and later into unity consciousness. This means god-consciousness is not marked by a distinct phase-shift in consciousness, like Self-realization is, but is rather a gradual fusion of void, bliss and Shakti. Unity consciousness it not marked by a clear shift in consciousness either, but is a phase that fluctuates.

112. When external non-duality becomes stable, god-consciousness transforms into unity consciousness.

As described in the previous verse, states beyond Self-realization fluctuate. Stabilizing in god-consciousness will lead to unity consciousness. God-consciousness is marked by perceiving Shakti in and as everything. Seeing Shakti in and as everything is the same as seeing Mother's grace in and as everything. Once this is stable, unity consciousness will gradually emerge.

> **113. Spanda is the dynamic throb of consciousness in which Shakti manifests as everything. Meditate on Spanda. Spanda is prior to Shakti in action. Thus everything is Shakti, which is the Divine Mother.**

Spanda is another word for Mother's grace. Technically Spanda is the primordial vibration of Shakti (Mother) from which creation springs (grace), hence everything in creation is Shakti. However, Spanda never ceases to be Shiva and Shakti and vice versa.

> **114. Meditation on Shiva first leads to void consciousness, then with difficulty to unity consciousness. Meditation on Shakti leads directly to god-consciousness, then with ease to unity consciousness.**

This throws some light on which path one may be inclined to follow. The path of the neo-Advaitin advocates meditation on Shiva (pure being), and it will lead to pure Self-realization, but will not lead to god-consciousness. Full enlightenment, then, is three steps away for a neo-Advaitin, while it is only two steps away for a Shakti-yogi who surrenders to a fully awakened kundalinī.

115. Meditate on the unity of Shiva and Shakti as your own Self. Simultaneously meditate on void and vibrant, blissful Shakti in the body.

In fact there is no difference between the two meditations and the distinction is merely for pedagogical reasons.

116. Peace is an illusion unless, at least in void consciousness, since it will eventually pass. In void consciousness peace acquires a completely different meaning since one is internally beyond conflict and beyond any kind of non-peace. Void, however, is not even to be called peace; it is simply devoid of everything; thus non-peace and peace are not relevant descriptors for Self-realization.

This means that peace can only be found when transcending everything. However, since one has transcended everything in Self-realization, there is no longer any conflict that could be resolved in peace.

117. Peace means something that could be in conflict is in harmony. Thus peace is based on duality and the term is not relevant with respect to the Self.

In the void of Self-realization, where one utterly and totally realizes peace, there can in fact not be said even to be peace, since peace implies duality and plurality in harmony.

118. The Self is even devoid of void-ness. The term void-consciousness is a metaphor describing basic Self-realization. Not until in unity consciousness has one fully realized the Self as non-void.

Void is inferior since it is anchored in the duality between unmanifest and manifest. Only when this duality goes away can one claim to be fully enlightened and this happens in unity consciousness.

119. After void, non-void culminates in the fullness of Mother. Then unity is close.

Intense bhakti (devotion to the supreme) characterizes one who has gone beyond void-consciousness into god-consciousness.

This devotion is the fullness of Mother. When totally absorbed in the fullness of Mother, unity will be close.

120. Ultimately Mother loses herself in you as the unity of Shakti and Shiva. Then you become highly contagious. Every breath becomes a love song to Mother and an outflow of Shakti.

This is a different way of describing losing the divine Mother. If your kundalinī-sādhana has been successful and you have reached into god-consciousness, you will become contagious and will be able to give shaktipāt.

121. While merged with the Self, surrender to Mother as Shakti in you. Even though you do not see Shakti as Mother, rest assured, Shakti is intelligent, compassionate and caring; hence we call Shakti "Mother".

If you are not quite so advanced on the path, rest assured that Mother's grace will be with you if you stick to your kundalinī-shaktipāt sādhana.

122. Devotion blossoms in radical non-duality. Meditate on this with feeling and heart and transcend the seeming paradox.

The seeming paradox is: you live in non-duality, yet you are devoted to Mother. So is there duality between you and Mother? No, not really and yes there is. This is a paradox that ultimately will be transcended through devotion. This devotion begins even before radical non-duality. It blossoms in god-consciousness and is fulfilled in unity consciousness.

123. While in radical devotion, which is radical surrender, one is being meditated on by Mother. Becoming the object of Mother's meditation is the highest sādhana. Without shaktipāt, this is not possible.

Such is divine grace that one does not have to lift a finger in order to become enlightened. However, this radical devotion, or para-bhakti, is not possible until you reach god-consciousness. It requires effort to get to god-consciousness. It is rarely possible without shaktipāt.

124. Shaktipāt is the initiation by which the recipient becomes the object of Mother's meditation. It may

**blossom quickly or slowly depending on the readiness of
the recipient.**

Amazingly as this may seem, it is quite true. When the grace of
Shakti descends on one for good, then one becomes the object of
the divine Mother's meditation. Not all who receive shaktipāt are
ready for this, but some are. It also depends on the state of the one
who gives shaktipāt. If he is not one with Mother, at least
temporarily, he cannot give it.

**125. Shaktipāt may be given in numerous ways and
under numerous circumstances. It may be given secretly
or openly. It may be given for numerous reasons or no
reason at all.**

Generally shaktipāt is given during a certain formal sitting where
you meditate together. But it may be given spontaneously for no
apparent reason. Also it may be given through an object, like a
rosary or a fruit. It can be given through touch, sight or merely
intent.

**126 As shaktipāt unfolds one becomes meditated on
rather than one performing meditation. This is a
peculiar process not known to any other sādhana. Thus**

shaktipāt sādhana is supreme sādhana. It is also known as siddha yoga or kundalinī maha yoga.

Once it sets in, it is a rather peculiar experience. Meditation becomes surrender to being meditated on by the divine. Siddha yoga means perfect yoga; maha yoga means the greatest yoga. It is called thus because all other yoga forms manifest spontaneously in the yogi through grace.

127. Once shaktipāt sādhana grabs you it will never leave you and will stay with you from one incarnation to the next. Thus shaktipāt sādhana is supreme love.

128. Once shaktipāt sādhana grabs you and you have become Self-realized, you will become contagious and others may receive shaktipāt from you. Thus shaktipāt sādhana is supreme grace.

129. Faith is not required. Once shaktipāt sādhana grabs you, you will know. This knowledge will become deeper and deeper until it merges with Mother.

How can one know if one has been grabbed by Shakti? There are several signs: meditation will become spontaneous and kriyās will occur. In meditation one will feel the surge of Shakti up the spine and it will feel like a million needle pricks in the hands and on the scull, or like ants crawling all over, or like a strong tingle in the skin. Bliss will come by itself and so will inner light during meditation. One will long for meditation.

130. Grace knows no boundaries; however the mind may set up barriers such as fear or doubt. Shakti will burn them away, which may provoke them for a while.

Fears and doubts and other boundaries may flare up in meditation, but that is just because they are in actual fact being burnt out of the system. Don't worry about such fits of emotion or doubt, just surrender to the Shakti and let it go on its way purifying you from within.

131. Reversing the flow of prāna gives rise to an increased sense of Shakti.

There are many ways to do this. Prānāyāmas are typically used. One such prānāyāma is to breath in to the count of three while sensing energy rush up the spine and into the brain; then hold the breath to the count of three sensing energy radiating from the brain in all directions; then breathe out to the count of three sensing energy radiating from the brain in all directions. Then breathe in again to the count of three, and so forth for as long as you like. This is kundalinī prānāyāma as described in verse 58.

132. Reverse the flow of prāna by feeling the energy body expand on the in-breath and contract on the out-breath.

133. Alternatively visualize and sense Shakti and love pouring into the spine and radiating from the spine at the same time.

If you find it difficult to get it into the spine, then just do it with the entire body.

134. As the sense of Shakti increases, surrender increases.

As one becomes filled with vibrant Shakti and bliss comes in meditation, it is natural to surrender to Shakti.

135. Surrender comes in three forms: Surrender to Shakti, surrender to Self and surrender to Mother. All

three are gifts of Mother Shakti. Mother, Shakti and Self are one.

First there is surrender to the grace operating in one as Shakti, then one surrenders to the Self and becomes Self-realized. One could remain in a state of Self-realization without moving forward, or one could move forward into devotion and surrender to the Divine Mother Shakti. You know you have moved from pure Self-realization into god-consciousness when you begin to see Shakti in everything as a vibrant immaterial energy and you also see a faint golden light permeating everything.

136. Love is the oil that makes surrender flow smoothly. It is not of sufficient quality or intensity unless kundalinī-shakti operates at or above the heart.

The wonder of this path is that what is needed for the path to flow smoothly is also given to you along the path. One does not have to sit passively, though, as the next verses show.

137. Open the heart by doing chakra prānāyāma at the centre of the chest.

Sense a ball of energy about an inch large in the chakra. Sense it expand on the in-breath and contract on the out-breath. Do this for ten breaths. Then sense the chakra radiate on both the in- and out-breath. Do this for ten breaths. Then sense the ball of energy moving forwards on the in-breath and backwards on the out-breath. Do this for ten breaths. That is one round. Do as many as you please.

138. When relating to others think of them as the Self or as Mother.

Actually this will come naturally at some point where everybody and even everything will be seen as Mother Shakti (in god-consciousness).

139. Raise Shakti to and above the heart by doing kundalinī-prānāyāma.

This prānāyāma is described in stanza 58.

140. As kundalinī rises above the heart, deeper and more nuanced shades of love unfold. Love is not limited to the heart; it only appears so when looking from below the heart.

141. When I-ness and objects of consciousness combine, personality arises. Thus personality is a conglomerate of objects of consciousness relating to each other through I-ness and I AM.

This is the secret of ignorance. It also shows that liberation does not consist in getting established in I AM or I-ness. One has to transcend I AM and I-ness and merge into the unmanifest Self.

142. Personality is based on I AM. I AM is based on I-ness. When I-ness is transcended, personality is transcended. Even though transcended, personality remains but without any identification with it.

So even though you are lucky to transcend I AM you still have to go beyond I-ness. I-ness is more subtle than I AM, and it is more like a subtle vibration in the field of pure being than it is a distinct something to be observed. It can be observed from the Self though, as basic self-referentiality, and should be if possible.

143. Good and bad traits of personality matter very little; they are equally distracting from the Self. They are equal impediments for realization.

It is important to be a decent person. But even a crook can become Self-realized if he works towards it. What is meant with this verse is that you need not fight yourself over your bad traits.

> **144. Realization is not a result of good or bad karma. Realization transcends karma. Good or bad karma tend to orient one towards or away from a spiritual life conducive to realization, but karma in itself does not give realization.**

So realization is not something you earn from being a good person doing good deeds.

> **145. Good karma fertilizes the soil; transcending karma plants the seed. Transcending karma is the same as transcending I AM and I-ness. The flower of Self-realization sprouts when identifications begin to go away; it blossoms in full realization where all identifications have gone and the identification principle in I-ness is transcended and dissolved.**

Once the identification principle has been transcended, you can truthfully say about your body and your mind: This is not me!

146. Personality is a complex network of manifesta-tions of Shakti relating to each other. This relating is dependent on the active presence of I AM. It hides pure being.

One part of the mind looks at another part of the mind and says: that is me. This other part of the mind, on the other hand, looks at a third part of the mind and says: that is me. And so on ad infinitum. There is no such thing as a personality that is you; it is a fiction, a construct with which you identify by being involved in the individual identifications and by being lost in its complexity.

147. Since personality is a network of Shakti manifestations it is ever changing and not the Self. There is no such thing as a personality essence which is really you.

Everything manifest is a manifestation of Shakti, so is the personality. The personality is in a state of flux and it continually changes. There is no such thing as a personality that is truly you. You are free, the personality is a prison of energy fluctuations woven together with I AM.

148. I AM is identified as the essence of one's personality, which is true, but it is not the Self; it is the seed of further fluctuations of consciousness that congeal to form personality.

I am this, I am that! As long as there is an I that is, there will be objects of identification. It is in theory possible to rest into the pure sense of I AM, but it will not have removed identifications and will thus not be freedom.

149. Realizing I AM is not a stable realization; it will be lost again as fluctuations of consciousness again hide it.

I AM not only contains all the latent identifications, but it is furthermore an unstable state.

150. Realizing the Self is a stable state since it is free of identifications and I-ness and I AM have been transcended. Thus the three gunas and karma have been transcended and only pure being remains in and as itself with full self-awareness.

Self-realization on the other hand, is a stable and irreversible state because it is free of I-ness. The three gunas are tamas, rajas and sattva, which somewhat can be translated as inertia, action and purity. The three gunas are considered to be the primal building forces behind everything created. One is not liberated until one has transcended the gunas. Transcending I-ness means transcending the gunas.

151. Self-awareness can be developed by transcending the gunas through habitually placing awareness in the Self. Thus I-ness is habitually transcended and identification gradually withdraws from the complex structure of illusory personality. However, withdrawal of identification has to be consciously practiced alongside conscious transcending. Awareness must become aware of freedom from identification for the identification principle to be transcended.

The three gunas and the I-ness operate on the same subtle level of nature. Just as I-ness is a subtle vibration, barely manifest, so are the gunas. Thus transcending the gunas and transcending I-ness amounts to the same thing. The three gunas are tendencies within the subtle vibration of māyā. Māyā operating on you as an individual person is I-ness. The gunas are manifestations of Shakti.

152. The identification principle is the inherent tendency of I AM to project I-ness onto inter-subjective manifestations of the gunas and their interrelationships. This tendency remains as long as I AM and I-ness are not transcended. A clear realization of I AM may temporarily and superficially look like Self-realization, but it will not last so it is not Self-realization.

What is here described is the complex of the personality, where one part identifies with another ad infinitum. It is not you. In I AM there will be something that resembles witnessing towards this complex, but it is not the real witnessing spoken of in relation to being established in the Self.

153. Self-realization will never go away. There is nowhere it can go and nothing that can occlude it.

Self-realization is irreversible. This is because the identification breaks down and goes away. Once free of it, it will never come back.

154. Self-realization can negatively be defined as freedom from I-ness.

258

155. The Self can never be positively defined, since it is utterly unmanifest.

The Self has no attributes, so it cannot be positively defined as this or that.

156. However, Self-realization can be described as awareness self-aware in and as the Self.

This is strictly speaking not a positive definition since the Self is void.

157. The Self can be negatively defined as pure being prior to any structure or fluctuation of consciousness and prior to any essence of personhood. Thus it is prior to I-ness and I AM.

I-ness is the primal vibration out of pure being from which personhood arises. I AM is the first illusory sense of self that springs from the vibration of I-ness.

158. Since the Self is utterly unmanifest awareness in and of itself it will be without an object. Thus any

meditation method will have to be transcended in order to reach the Self. This is radical letting go.

Meditation is like taking a train ride. If you don't get off the train at the right station, you have missed your destination. Similarly, any valid practice for getting realized will have to have built into it the option for letting go of the practice at the right time.

159. Letting go can be practiced within the domain of I AM or within the domain of the Self; be very aware of which domain you are operating in. I AM realization is without bliss.

Bliss is one of the things that mark unity with the Self. However, bliss means many things. The first type of bliss of which I am speaking has a number of associated phenomena like a wildly beating heart and flickering eyelids as well as strong inner light. This is first stage of spiritual bliss, known as ecstasy.

160. Letting go within I AM will lead to a sense of oneness with one's essence. This essence is an illusion, but is not seen as such in this kind of realization.

161. Letting go within the domain of the Self will lead to oneness with void and supreme uncaused bliss.

Letting go is not in itself a valid parameter for the quality of one's meditation. Letting go into I AM will fool many a person to believe it is letting go into the Self, however, it is not. Uncaused bliss only comes when it is the Self you surrender to; in I AM there is no bliss, only a sense of pleasant emptiness.

162. I AM does not know supreme bliss, only beingness combined with a sense of "I". I AM does not know the supreme void of basic Self-realization. Void Self-realization is also without bliss. Be aware that I AM-ness and the Self can be confused while transcending without bliss.

This makes things difficult: It is actually possible to achieve a Zen-like enlightenment which is characterized by pure being and absolutely no bliss. However, in such an enlightenment there is no kundalinī involved, hence no Shakti, and it is a dry state.

163. Shakti is the supreme guide since it takes one through the void to supreme bliss.

Shakti will take one to a higher state of enlightenment than plain Self-realization. After Self-realization comes god-consciousness and then unity consciousness and those stuck in plain Self-realization will have a hard time getting there. One way to be stuck in plain Self-realization is to dismiss everything else as an experience and thus as invalid; for example to dismiss kundalinī and Shakti as mere energy phenomena without spiritual value; and so forth.

164. Supreme bliss is the direct recognition of the Self as Shakti in other.

This is a higher state of bliss than the one mentioned earlier that was ecstatic. This is the bliss of god-consciousness, the state of enlightenment that lies beyond Self-realization.

165. Separateness arises with I-ness and I AM and culminates in identification with personality.

Recognition of the Self as Shakti in other, and the notion that personality is the self, marks two very different states of consciousness. The one described here is the structure of individual ignorance as seen from the perspective of Self-realization.

166. When I AM is transcended and one is in void, then one feels separate from everything since one has lost identification and sees identification all around; however, there is no longer identification with anyone separate, thus separateness is not an issue as such.

Only when one is free of identification does one see clearly how everyone and everything around one is caught up in identifications. Void-realization can be lonely until one moves on and recognizes Shakti in others.

167. Only when lovebliss arises from Shakti does separateness go away. You feel not only connected with everything, you see your beloved Shakti in and as everything.

Again, we have here stepped up to god-consciousness beyond Self-realization.

168. Ultimately everything is seen as the Self and seen as Shakti. Self and Shakti are one.

Here we have stepped up into unity-consciousness

169. Thus all is Mother Shakti.

Even in unity consciousness supreme devotion remains. However, you are one with mother Shakti at this point, unlike in god-consciousness, where there was a duality between you and the divine.

QUESTIONS

Kundalini Tantra

What Place does Love Play in Self-Realization?

Question: In your opinion, what place does love of an "object" play in Self-realization?

Jan: Devotion is very important and devotion is centered on love of an "object". But what is an "object"? One has to be devoted to the Self, devoted to the highest truth and devoted to god in love. In fact the three should merge into one as one progresses and should merge with one's devotion into a vibrant field of Shakti that one senses pouring into and radiating from the body. Once one reaches that stage of sādhana (spiritual practice), devotion to god and love of any object will be one, and more or less permanent as it penetrates one throughout body, mind and heart with longing and love. One becomes focused on Self-realization 24/7 and everyday life becomes sādhana. In fact this kind of love/devotion/Shakti will take you beyond mere Self-realization.

Question: The crux of my teacher's teaching for the last few years has been personal love as the fastest way to Self-realization. All of this is because he said he was a dried up Jnāni for several years, then this student came along who had a lot of energies and passions, he fell in love with her...this relationship that he had with her became the center of all his teachings. He tried, using his power as guru, to get her to leave her husband and two children, as he often told her and others of his students that unless their marriages were falling apart and they lost their jobs and became totally dysfunctional that there was something wrong with their practice.

Jan: Excuse me, but this sounds nasty and dirty. It sounds like your teacher has a problem with his base desires. First he denies them and dries up, then he is overwhelmed by them and tries to ruin someone else's marriage for the sake of his own libido gratification. Then he justifies his libido by reformulating his teachings to suit it. No, marriages should not fall apart and one should not lose one's job and one should not become dysfunctional to be sure one's practice is correct. Self-realization is a matter of disidentification, not of functionality or dysfunctionality.

Question: This is only a wee small bit of what I am trying to come out of. I cannot do this without you. I have friends that say, "just trust yourself...and..." but I know that I can trust myself, whatever that means, for eons...and that identification still be there.

Jan: Self-trust is good, but irrelevant with respect to getting Self-realized. It is of the ego which one is in the process of letting go of. In fact, loss of self-trust may be an issue prior to Self-realization as one learns to witness the ego and sees its illusory nature.

Question: What does it take to end this I AM-ness once and for all? Is this just a pure act of grace? Or of diligent practice...which is also an act of grace it seems?

Jan: You can get to I AM by self-effort through meditation, inquiry and introspection. The last bit beyond that is grace and luck.

Surrender

Question: Could you speak about surrender?

Jan: Basically bliss or Shakti wells up and you let go and merge with it. That is surrender. Surrender to external deities is not real surrender; that is just a nice mood. Surrender should be internal; to the Self. If you surrender to Shakti within it will take you to the Self. Then you surrender to pure being and merge into samādhi. See, surrender is essential all the way. Without surrender you won't make it.

Question: What about surrender in love to a partner?

Jan: There can be a heart opening in that, but it will not take you to the Self.

Question: I thought love was the highest?

Jan: No, not as such. There are many levels of love. There is physical love, sexual love, partner love, spiritual love and spiritual compassion. There are more kinds of love than can be listed, but basically the love that transcends the physical is more profound. Partner love is usually physical in that the body is required for it; it does not have to be sexual to be physical if you identify your partner with his or her body and vice versa.

Question: What about in Self-realization? What is love like then?

Jan: Pure Self-realization is very idealistic about love, but pure Self-realization is not such a high state; we are aiming higher. The love in God-realization is really profound. Self-realization is really just void and there is not much love in it because of the realization. There can be all the usual kinds of love, of course, but one tends to be idealistic about it in Self-realization.

Question: What about God-consciousness?

Jan: In God consciousness there is a different kind of love altogether. It transcends the physical and is a direct relationship with the divine in everything.

Question: I see God in everything; everything as divine.

Jan: No, you are seeing a concept of God in everything. You are projecting an idea onto the world. You don't get to God-consciousness without Self-realization.

Question: But I surrender to this divine I see in everything.

Jan: That is not the kind of surrender we are speaking of now. That is surrender to a concept, a notion, a mood. What we are after is surrender to the Self. You can't properly surrender to God unless Shakti is awakened in you and you are in God-consciousness.

Kundalinī and Self-Realization

Question: The lovebliss occurs to whom or what? Is this an unconditioned, source essence without subject or object?

Jan: The lovebliss IS the Self, it occurs to no one. But the body/mind complex enjoys the suffusion of Shakti that occurs when one is "in" the lovebliss state. It is indeed unconditioned and prior to subject/object. It is the Self. The Self is Sat-Chit-Ānanda; ānanda means bliss or lovebliss.

Question: If unconditioned, why the condition of kundalinī in the brain? Why the dependent link to anything of the human (even if it be astral or other subtle energy) body?

Jan: Kundalinī in the brain is important; it transforms the body/mind complex so it can uphold the high state. You can get Self-realized without this transformation, but then you will not have the Shakti and the bliss, it will just be void. You have to understand that kundalinī-shakti is one with the Shakti, the Self. Kundalinī is not some separate astral energy. Kundalinī is the manifestation of you as an individual ignorant being. Kundalinī has built you up as you are now and kundalinī runs the show, because kundalinī is the Shakti of the Self in a condensed or crystallized form metaphorically speaking. So kundalinī is the key to your ignorance and also the key to your full enlightenment. You have to get kundalinī to operate in the reverse direction of what it normally operates; that is, you have to "awaken" it as we say. An unawakened kundalinī may send its energy to the heart or brain and you will then have an experience of bliss that lasts as long as it lasts, but it will pass and just be a nice memory. An awakened kundalinī will transform your body and your ego-mind to be able to uphold the state of full enlightenment (sat-chit-ānanda); then bliss states act as magnets pulling you into the Self. You have to get rid of kundalinī as such in order to reach full enlightenment, and you get rid of kundalinī in the brain when kundalinī gets absorbed into Shiva (pure Being).

Question: Linking lovebliss to kundalinī in the brain appears to make lovebliss just another human experience of bodily energies – though they be highly subtle ones.

Jan: It is not a matter of having experiences. The bliss is the Self and it is all about getting Self-realized. The effect of getting kundalinī into the brain is that Shakti is fully awake in your system and is pulling you into the Self. So when is it an experience? You have to ask this. As long as you are not Self-realized, any samādhi can be classified as an experience since it is temporary, even void or satori. Any temporary contact with the Self from a Shakti point of view (kundalinī in the brain), will be full of lovebliss, and this bliss will pull your mind out of its

274

current stuff and into the Self. You can classify the initial bliss as an experience, since it is temporary, but it has high value in terms of speeding up your sādhana and making your sādhana immensely joyful. Sādhana without Shakti, is dry and barren; it is like trying to grow a tree without watering it. You need to awaken kundalinī, or rather get it to operate upwards, back to source (the Self), rather than downwards towards ego. If you get kundalinī into the brain and it is not awakened, kundalinī will come down again and you will be no wiser for that experience. If kundalinī is awakened and not only reaches the brain, but merges with Shiva/Pure Being there, then you have undone your egoic structure completely and merged with the Self. Then there is no question of it being an experience (temporary) because you will be One with the Self, which is Shiva-Shakti and pure bliss.

Question: Wouldn't such linked lovebliss get left behind when the body/personality-self is transcended that is made up in part of kundalinī energy and brain?

Jan: When you leave your body, if your kundalinī is awakened, you will not leave the bliss behind, but will merge into it and probably get Self-realized. If not ready to get Self-realized at death, you will - as you always do - take kundalinī with you as your essence and out of it a new form will manifest as a new birth/life/personality. But it is not that you take kundalinī with you like a dog on a leash, you have to understand that you are kundalinī. Kundalinī is your essence; it is you as an ignorant individual. You have to deconstruct that. Kundalinī is a manifestation of pure Shakti, which is the Self.

God-Consciousness

Question: Let me tell you about an experience. My whole reality changed, or I could say reality got a plus to it. A kind of energy was emanating from my pure being. Everybody got centered on me and I saw the Self in their eyes. What do I mean with god-realization? Well first it felt like my "I" burnt out completely. This lasted for 2 months and was very painful. When I couldn't bear the pain anymore I visited a psychologist. I told him I feel that I am losing all my memories, my name and everything. To be honest I thought I would end up as a vegetable. The psychologist told me that I was losing my ego, not my memories and that it was a pre-psychotic state. It was like a nirvikalpa samādhi in a fluid and dynamic way where my worldly awareness remained. When all pain vanished and I was completely relaxed, a vision (a golden light without form) appeared in my mind in a flash. It was like a picture but first I was so blissed and relaxed that I couldn't comprehend it but later I remembered it. After the vision something flooded me and I cried: "I am God". God realized God in me!

Jan: This sounds like an authentic experience, not something "pre-psychotic". I recognize much of what you are saying. After one nirvikalpa samādhi I was so empty of ego I could not even remember "my" own name and memories were gone. This lasted until next morning – meanwhile my guru helped me get some identity back. You don't become like a vegetable, you are totally free, that's all. But is it not a practical state, it is good to preserve some ego to function in the world; the art is to not be identified with that remaining bit of ego.

When one realizes the divine, one has to be very humble about it. True, there is oneness, but if there is a crying out of "I am god" that is the ego crying out and the oneness is not complete. When you are one with God, there is no one to say he is one with God. Also it is not "God realizing god in me"; God is already perfectly and totally Self-realized, that is the nature of God. God does not suddenly realize God in you, God already is in full realization and this full realization may partly dawn on you too, as in the experience you are describing. It will appear as if something greater than you come to realize itself in and as you, but in reality it is the Self that reveals its nature to you. This revelation is the grace of the Divine Mother Shakti. In the heat of the moment, the mind will grab onto what it can, and that is to understand what is happening as the grace of God. Which it is, but it is also freedom from God and oneness with the Self. It is not "God realizing God"; it is the Self ceasing to act as if ignorant by the grace of the Divine Mother Shakti.

It sounds like you have had an aroused kundalinī. The "kind of energy emanating from your pure being" is Shakti: The Divine Mother as the energy of the pure being. This radiates from one when one has been blessed by Mother with an active kundalinī-shakti. Others will feel it and one will be able to see Shakti in others eyes. The recognition will be experienced as recognition of the divine in other, which it to some degree is, since it is the Divine Mother at play. One will also see everything as emptiness and see the pure being in others as void.

After such experiences, or periods, one usually enters a phase of painful emptiness as the Shakti recedes and there is only void left. The remedy to this is devotion to Shakti and this is expressed in meditation on her presence in you as kundalinī. The meditations under How to Meditate are designed for this and I recommend you try them for a period of time.

When the Divine first breaks into one's awareness it usually happens with a bang. This contrasts starkly with the void of merging with pure being. It is important not to value one realization higher than the other. God-realization may begin before one is Self-realized or it may begin after. Spiritual evolution is not a set linear thing. Glimpses of God-realization before one is Self-realized does not mean one is closer to basic Self-realization than one who has never had a glimpse of the divine. So be humble.

Question: I have heard of sahaja samādhi what do you know about it?

Jan: Sahaja samādhi is a natural and spontaneous state of

samādhi. It is Self-realization. It is permanent and stable. Actually there are many levels of sahaja samādhi: Self-realization, God realization, Unity Consciousness, etc. Some reserve the phrase sahaja samādhi to the highest final samādhi and I respect that. This is how David Spero uses it, for example.

Question: What is the difference between nirvikalpa and sahaja samādhi?

Jan: Nirvikalpa samādhi is temporary. Here you are absorbed completely in the void of pure being and become unconscious. Ego and sense of self recede totally. Savikalpa samādhi is also temporary; it is conscious samādhi where ego remains functional. In sahaja samādhi, ego remains functional, but there is absolutely no identification with it at all. You are free. You are one with the Self and nothing can disturb this, because the mechanism of separation, the I AM-ness, has gone away. Sahaj samādhi is permanent, the others are temporary.

Question: Is it true that the process which begins with god-realization is irreversible?

Jan: Yes, what has begun with the grace of God will come to fruition someday. If God has cast his/her glance on you, you are in his/her grace and he/she will not let you go. I guess what you have experienced is the Divine Mother acting upon you, so let's say "she". Mother's grace is infallible. If you receive it, it will ripen no matter what you do. You can slow it down or speed it up but it will manifest in you without fail.

Question: In my opinion one doesn't need to get rid of the ego, more it must be illuminated, do you agree?

Jan: The ego does not get illuminated more and more; that is a misconception promoted by New Age and Rudolf Steiner's Anthroposophy and similar groups. The truth is you become less and less identified with ego. Ego does not need to go away; you just realize more and more it is not you. However, with time and sahaja samādhi it does go more and more away, but I doubt it vanishes altogether, for then you would not even know your name nor have memories. I have been in this completely ego-less and memory-less state and it is a great freedom, but not very practical. It is better to see the ego as Shakti at play, as the grace of Mother; then living with it will be a life of bliss. This, by the way, is our version of sahaja samādhi. There is also a sahaja samādhi devoid of bliss which the Advaita Vedāntins reach. Ours is more fun though, since it is a huge love affair with the Divine Mother and it also encompasses the void of the Advaita Vedāntins. In both cases one has ridden oneself of identifications altogether and also got rid of the I AM-ness, the seed of ignorance, but to the Vedāntin the ego/mind is just empty illusion; to us the ego/mind is dynamic Shakti, which is love-bliss.

Question: isn't the end goal I AM THAT?

Jan: I AM THAT is a sad ending to a beautiful journey. It should end with love-bliss. I AM THAT is void, pure and simple. Our goal is to enliven the void as well as the relative with the grace of the Divine Mother and indeed to merge with that grace.

Question. What is devotion and what place does it have?

Jan: Devotion comes in two varieties: bhakti and parabhakti. Bhakti is a mood and parabhakti is a natural state of enlightenment.

Question: What is parabhakti like?

Jan: You are on fire with love of the divine, of God, of Shakti, of the divine mother. The body and mind become vibrating fields of what I call lovebliss, and this is hot and soft and sweet at the same time. It sucks you into love, yet there is nothing left to suck in because you are one. It is totally paradoxical. Every breath you take is a song of love for the divine mother. You see the divine mother in everything around you and this melts your heart. It is total surrender to Shakti. Shakti burns you up and the fusion of Shakti and love ensures that those who sit with you become transformed and their Shakti awakens also. When this happens, you realize again and again that they and you are one in love and surrender. You do not pray anymore, because mother is showering her grace on you every moment. You are afire with her grace and this fire is contagious. You are drunk on love. Need I go on?

Question: No, this is fine. What place does parabhakti have in one's sādhana?

Jan: When you are ripe, it will come by itself. Then you will know. To get it you should get kundalinī shakti going and surrender to Shakti.

I AM is Thick as a Brick. Pure Being is Prior

Question: For quite a while now I've had access to the self ... or rather the "I AM".

Jan: Don't confuse those two. I AM is not the Self. I'll explain below.

Question: You speak of bliss. Bliss has never really been part of my experience. For me it's just the pure is-ness, it's more serene than anything else.

Jan: Bliss and serenity are odd terms used to signify so much. You speak of pure is-ness and I AM. But pure is-ness is prior to I AM. In pure is-ness, there is no "I" that "IS", hence no I AM. I AM is a gross state that does resemble the absolute state of pure being, but is has a subtle ignorance at its core. In pure and primal is-ness you are void. This void is serene, but devoid of paramānanda (what I called bliss or lovebliss). In this void, you experience everything else as illusion (māyā). However at a higher state of development you recognize the pure being and is-ness in and as everything else, hence māyā is not just transcended internally, but also externally, and this recognition is supremely blissful. Just because

284

you have not experienced this supreme bliss (paramānanda) it does not mean your serenity is higher "than anything else", it just means you have not experienced paramānanda. Paramānanda is a very high state and very few reach it. It is beyond pure IS-ness and utterly incomprehensible for those who have not experienced it. It is a love relationship with God where you and God merge into One-Love-Bliss.

Question: And how to transcend the "I AM"? Or is it a natural progression of constant self-remembrance till one realizes the "I AM" is not It? And one is then able to see what is behind that?

Jan: Self-remembrance leads to the I AM state, and no further. Once fairly established in the I AM-ness, your awareness can fold back in on itself and short circuit, so to speak. But the step from I AM to pure being is best taken by grace and Shakti. It is so easy to get stuck in I AM and think you have reached the goal – and it usually needs a helping hand to get beyond that. In I AM-ness you are a witness to everything exterior including all levels of the mind and ego, except I-ness. But the final wipe out of ignorance has not taken place, there is still an I that believes it IS and it claims to be the Self, but it is not. In basic Self-realization, this sense goes away also and there is just serene void. Self-realization is prior to soul. Soul-realization is realizing one's I AM-ness.

Question: How does one get access to the "Self" and not the I AM?

Jan: Access to I AM is not access to the Self. It is access to "a higher self", but not The Self. You can use I AM as a doorway, but it is easy to get stuck there. If I AM is a door, it is more likely to be shut than to be open. Shaktipāt and kundalinī are the best ways to open it. Access to Self rather than I AM is best achieved by "riding" on a surge of Shakti since Shakti is the Self. This usually requires shaktipāt (kundalinī-awakening through grace). If you, however, can experience awareness as pure being-energy and let awareness become fully aware of itself, then you can momentarily snap out of I AM-ness and into pure being, or is-ness.

Question: I guess it's a bit hard to put into words as there is no observer. In explaining my state, I'll put it bluntly, the mind has stopped, if thoughts arise they are transparent and the mechanism which refers to them is also transparent. The experience is expansive. Where "I" begin and creation starts isn't clear, it's almost a feeling of oneness. This is the height of the experience during regular waking hours. If I engage too much with my environment I lose it to a certain degree. However, I can rather easily come back to this state.

Jan: Very good. You are close to basic Self-realization. You just need to get rid of the subtle identification.

Question: My kundalinī experience is minimal. Few experiences, energy flows, root chakra stirring, but I highly doubt that it is fully awakened. Any recommendations as to heighten receptivity?

Jan: Try the kundalinī prānāyāma. Here it is:

1. Breathe in to the count of three. Sense energy rising up the spine to the brain.

2. Hold your breath to the count of three. Sense energy radiating from the brain in all directions.

3. Breathe out to the count of three. Sense energy radiating from the brain in all directions.

Repeat.

It is important to find a nice and relaxed tempo so you can keep at it uninterrupted for 45 minutes. If bliss comes or shakti fills your body with love, just surrender to it and merge. I promise you will get results.

(Another questioner enters the discussion)

Question: I am stuck with this situation of witnessing I AM. It's weird. If we talk about the observer from mind, I think that this observer comes along with every new thought. New thought, new observer. Then I figured that this observer maybe is attention.

Jan: There are two observers:

1. The mind.

2. Pure being.

This means "observing the observer" has two states:

1. Awareness observing the mind observing. This is a trap.

2. Pure being observing its reflection in and as awareness. This is not a trap.

Question: Do you mean that those two are two different observations, or are they the same?

Jan: Two different observations. The seeker gets confused because he can't distinguish between them.

Question: Yes. The second one?

Jan: The second one is pure awareness. There are two objects of awareness, which are:

1. Mind as observer. - This is where people usually get stuck in the belief they are "observing the observer".

2. Pure awareness. - This is the interesting one.

Question: The second one, is this the ultimate observer or is there even one more, the witnessing of all? Is this second one, pure being observing its reflection in and as the minds awareness, this witnessing of I Am?

Jan: The second one. Well, you should understand the two:

1. Pure being observing restricted awareness observing itself.
2. Pure being observing unrestricted awareness.

In the first you have I AM observing what "I" is. In the second you are reflexively observing that which is prior to I AM.

Question: It seems I am in the first.

Jan: Yes, you are struggling with the first level.

Question: Yes I guess. I know there is sometimes a kind of experience... When I see thoughts flowing.

Jan: To rephrase:

A. Experiencing the mind experience. This is where most get stuck.

B. Experiencing the experiencing of the mind as such. This is prior to A. This is where the more fortunate get stuck.

C. Experiencing the experiencer of the experiencing mind. This is prior to B. This is where we want to be. It ends here because here awareness folds in on itself and realizes its nature as the Self or pure being.

Question: Sometimes I am absorbed in a thought, and I don't know anything. Then in an instance I am aware that I am not absorbed in the thought anymore, and there is just nothing, just blank! When thought vanishes it seems like only I Am is there and thought is gone, so also the observer of that thought is also gone.

Jan: Yes, this sounds like reaching I AM – or level B just described. When experiencing the mind experience, and then minds experience stops, you are left with I AM. I AM is the anchor point from where awareness experiences the mind experiencing.

Question: But still there is an observer of "I AM", and this is mind-observer as well.

Jan: Hmmm... that is unfortunate; you are stuck in a loop.

Question: Yes, maybe. I think there is some concept I have to let go of... Maybe I expect something to happen...

Jan: Let go of the idea that you have to witness something.

Question: Yes, I agree to this. I think I have to continue doing this introspection... to just stay in and watch the automatic flow of thoughts.

Jan: No, watch that which watches thoughts. Try to short-circuit it all.

Question: But it feels like a mind-observer is created every time the attention goes to a thought.

Jan: Yes. You should reach level C described above.

Question: Is this an intuitive feeling, to try to watch the watcher?

Jan: Yes.

Question: Hmmm, I know that there is something... I think I know what you mean. It's just a very, very tiny veil separating me and the realization.

Jan: Yes! Try this:

1. Watch the thoughts.

2. Watch the watching of thoughts.

3. Hone in on the personality observing and being observed.

4. Observe both personalities (observed and observing) and realize they are two sides of a coin. The point you are observing from is I AM.

5. Observe I AM as a fiction, a fantasy.

6. Stop observing and be the pure being looking at personality.

If you then jump back into personality observing, observe that personality and start over. This is a very tricky practice. I hope it makes sense.

Question: OK, so when I am aware that there is a thought, then the watcher is there automatically. I know I am aware of the thought and identifying with it.

Jan: No, I am trying to describe a different practice. Focus on PERSONALITY rather than thought or observer. Just above I

AM, personality occurs, and when I AM identifies with personality then all is lost. I AM can be said to be the primal identification. If you can see behind this restriction, you are home.

Question: OK this is interesting! I feel this is kind of a new ground and it's very good; I feel not sure about the practice. This means I have to "see" something new! So when there is no thought in particular, what is there then?

Jan: Unmanifest personality.

Question: Aha, so there is personality! Is this the I AM?

Jan: It is slightly after, there is no personality in I AM. But the distinction is so subtle it means nothing.

Question: Can "I AM" also be the observer? I mean in the sense of pure awareness?

Jan: Not really, I AM is thick as a brick, so to speak. It is really a kind of voidish, subtle self without much form.

Question: Ahaaaa, this is very important to me!

Jan: Personality can observe. When I AM and personality get mixed, you have ego.

Question: But where is personality "born" or located?

Jan: I AM wants to be something, so mind offers its dubious services. This is the birthplace of personality.

Question: OK, so then personality is also thick as a brick?

Jan: Yes, absolutely.

Selected Bibliography

Deutsch, Eliot: <u>Advaita Vedānta: A Philosophical Reconstruction</u>, Hawaii UP. 1973 (1969).

Deutsch, Eliot, ed.: <u>The Essential Vedānta</u>, World Wisdom 2004.

Dyczkowski, Mark S. G.: <u>The Aphorisms of Shiva</u>, State University of New York Press, USA 1992.

Krivocheine, Basil (Archbishop): <u>In the Light of Christ – St. Symeon the New Theologian</u>, St. Vladimir's Seminary Press, New York, USA 1986.

Lakshmanjoo, Swami: <u>Shiva Sutras</u>, Universal Shaiva Fellowship, USA 2002.

Langford, Michael: <u>The most Rapid and Direct Means to Eternal Bliss</u>, The Freedom Religion Inc. 4th ed. 2006 (1998).

Muktānanda, Swami: <u>Siddha Meditation</u>, SYDA Foundation, USA 1982 (1977).

Ramānanda, swami (transl.): <u>Tripura Rahasya</u>. World Wisdom, USA 2002 (1959).

Singh, Jaideva (transl.): <u>Siva Sūtras</u>, Motilal Banarsidass, India 1982 (1979).

Singh, Jaideva: <u>Vedānta and Advaita Shaivagama of Kashmir, A Comparative Study</u>, Ramakrishna Mission Institute of Culture, India 2010 (1985).

Tigunait, Pandit Rajmani (transl.): <u>Shakti Sadhana, A Translation of the Tripura Rahasya</u>, Himalayan Institute Press, 2008 (1999).

Waite, Dennis: <u>The Book of One, The Spiritual Path of Advaita</u>, O-Books, England 2003.